One step at a time

Envisioning children for revival

Foreword by Daphne Kirk

Peter Smith

kevin mayhew

To God be the glory and thanks.
Without his vision, none of this would
ever have happened.

Foreword

Some people are prepared to take risks to pursue a vision.

Peter is one of those people!

Two years ago he made contact with me; we met on several occasions and eventually he sold his home, with no employment to go to and moved with his family so that he could more freely live out the passion in his heart.

That passion is to see a generation released to be all that God has called them to be! A Holy Spirit-filled army of children.

This book is about taking a fresh look at your vision for children; it will challenge mindsets and give you the opportunity of taking risks.

Peter can ask you to do this because he has done it himself and to me that is the greatest recommendation of all!

Hold on to your seatbelts!

Daphne Kirk

Acknowledgements

A special thank-you to my best friend, partner and co-worker throughout this adventure – my wife Jackie; the 'Generators', with whom we have been able to move from the theoretical to the practical! If it's in this book – they've 'been there and done that'. To my youngest son, Nathan – who is one of the Generators, and so has walked the walk with us, growing in the Lord as a result.

Finally, to Daphne Kirk who has been our close friend and mentor throughout this journey.

How it all started

The car that finally stopped was a Citroen CV5. For those of you who don't know what a CV5 looks like, it's a bit like a small, round-topped box on wheels. The young man driving it was quite large, and was accompanied by his girlfriend. The back seat was already occupied by a double bass in a large wooden box! Why had he stopped? Obviously he was showing his pity for the poor honeymoon couple standing in front of him, each being weighed down by a huge rucksack which was doing its best to drag them over backwards, and wistfully seeking a lift to the next campsite! Jackie and I looked at each other as we contemplated sharing the space in this, the very smallest of cars – with a large man, a normal-sized female, *and* a huge double bass. Plus, of course, our two large rucksacks! However, the charming driver's sympathy was not wasted. He had the key to our successful journey. He simply unzipped the roof of his car and stuck the long end of his double bass case out through the hole he had created in the roof, and allowed us to bury ourselves on the hitherto undiscovered half of the back seat under our camping gear. I can't say that this was the most comfortable journey we ever had, but it was certainly one we remembered.

We had seen the size and shape of the car as it slowed down, and in our minds the whole venture was impossible! The driver had other ideas. He turned the impossible into the possible by removing the constraints that we had seen. He lifted the roof!

Children's ministry is a bit like that CV5. For many years we have become so used to seeing our children constrained by the restrictions of the car, that we don't recognise the possibility of removing the roof!

After 10 years of running a Sunday school and countless years of involvement in one, Jackie and I were walking home one evening in September 1998 and considering how successfully our children had reduced our carefully conceived activities to dustbin fodder when she announced that she felt dry. Our classes were not going anywhere and we needed a rest. Then God spoke! I very rarely contradict my wife. After 25 years I have learned that when she comes to such a conclusion she is usually right! This time, however, I am certain that God spoke, and what he said through me was, 'No! – It is not *you* who are "dry" – it is the *material* you are using.' Now that was a really challenging thought!

We spent some time considering different materials but came to a very simple conclusion. In essence all the different books did was to present similar material in slightly different ways at a cost that was directly proportional to the quality of printing used. In effect they were all the same! How could we present the children with a visionary Sunday school if no suitable material seemed to be available? No suitable books? How could we have Sunday school without books?

Until this revelation, 'church' for us had been the same as it possibly is in many churches nationwide. A few hymns, a children's story – usually the most enjoyable part of the service for the adults too – then the 'children's' hymn would accompany their retreat to another place so that 'real church' could carry on without them. The children would then have their story. This often bore little or no resemblance to the message given in 'church' before their departure, and then the children would embark on the main task of the morning. This could be a nice exciting task like colouring a picture . . . or making something or other to remind them of the story.

If your children are anything like mine, the colouring or craft product is usually placed somewhere under the myriad of other craft *objets d'art* in the junk room that usually doubles as a bedroom at night time. Items are sometimes found if Mum suddenly remembers on Saturday evening that there was a connected verse to be learned. Otherwise they remain lost to the world until they are finally discovered flattened under the Lego boxes three months later! Now there is a lesson – any worthwhile Sunday school craft activity can be reduced to a pancake if left in the 'care' of a small boy for more than one day!

Now don't get me wrong on this. I have nothing against traditional Bible stories. I believe they provide a very valuable foundation for children to build their lives on. In their early years my three boys had a Bible story read to them every night as part of their evening 'storytime'. Jesus was always telling stories to illustrate his point. But, Jesus did more than just telling stories!

We then went through a few weeks during which coincidences far outran probability. Every day or so Jackie was given an 'insight' into another aspect of working with the children's groups. At the same time I had finally started reading a book I had been given over a month previously – *Children of Revival* by Pastor Vann Lane.* Every time Jackie had an 'insight', she would confront me with her thoughts, and usually I would have read that day about a very similar situation that had happened in Pensacola and how Pastor Lane had dealt with it. There were so many coincidences that we both started looking at Sunday school in a different way.

At this time some work we were doing with another Christian group brought us into contact with a family running a Sunday school in another part of the city. When we compared notes we found that they had been given a very similar vision for their work only weeks before us.

They had some initial difficulties as some of their teachers felt that they could not cope without the security of books. However, they finally decided to give the idea a trial.

Unfortunately, many Sunday school teachers have become so set in their ways that the concept of Sunday school work without books requires a conceptual realignment with which they cannot cope. As a result, churches attempting to step out in this new direction can expect opposition from some workers. It's all down to insecurity. If you have a book with every lesson set out, complete with each activity and colouring – you can't go wrong! That may be true, but it is also very difficult to progress beyond the limits set on paper – and where does God fit into the equation?

Most of the teachers we worked with decided to stay with set books simply because, to our knowledge, no one else had tried anything like this before – otherwise there would have been a book about it!

After the decision was taken to stay with the 'safe' and traditional methods of teaching, my wife and I felt disappointed, and as we walked home I suddenly felt that God was saying, 'This is like Caleb. You are like Joshua and Caleb. Joshua and Caleb saw the Promised Land for what it was. Others only saw the potential problems and refused to step out in faith. Consequently, only the children born in the desert actually entered it with them!' None of the Jews who left Egypt with Moses were allowed into the Promised Land.

At this time we had the chance to visit a major international church, so naturally we went. On the first day we were there a member of the ministry team stopped praying over us and after a few moments of quiet kept repeating 'Caleb! Caleb!' He said that God kept giving him this one name over and over again. Did the name Caleb mean anything to us?

**Children of Revival* (or *Letting Little Ones Lead*) Vann Lane, Destiny Image Publishers Inc., 1998

On the Sunday we were there we asked if we could go to their Sunday school to see what they were doing. We hoped that we might see a Sunday school like Pastor Lane's in action, however, we were shown the books the classes were using.

When we expressed our surprise that they were using books, the superintendent commented that the books were about to be phased out, as they believed God wanted the children to be taught without books.

We were now faced with an unusual situation. At least four churches scattered around the world had each been given a similar vision for their Sunday school. The vision involved a radical review of how Sunday school should be 'taught'. Although the main vision was the same in each case, the application was different, as each church situation is different, and it is obviously wrong for a church or Sunday school to copy exactly what another church is doing – using a method like a secret formula for success.

However, there have been a number of common elements in each of these four churches:

1. Certain passages of Scripture have suddenly carried more weight than ever before. The one that has reduced several teachers to tears has been Matthew 19:14. 'Let the little children come to *me*, and do not hinder them . . .' (NIV, my italics) In other words – do not get in the way! *I* want *my* children to come to *me!* That was a word of prophecy given at this time.
2. Some established teachers have not been able to cope with the vision and have expressed a desire to leave the teaching team.
3. Initially some churches tried to reject the vision. Visions are given to prophets, and a prophet is rarely accepted in his own town.
4. The leaders given the vision came under attack.

Despite all this, I believe this vision has been given to a number of churches for a very important reason.

God wants his children back. He doesn't want them to just be told stories *about* him, he actually wants to draw his children to himself. For years we have been teaching children *about* God, much as the religious teachers had been doing to the children of Israel prior to Jesus' ministry. Jesus gave the people of his day the chance to meet with God through his presence on earth. He also left his Holy Spirit so that all of us could also have direct access to God. And what do we do? We actively prevent children from having direct access – and yet Jesus told us that unless we approach God like little children . . . !

This gives us two very challenging thoughts.

First we need our children to show us the way to reach God. They could be the key the Church needs to unlock the blessings that I believe God wants to pour into his Church . . . and what are we doing with the key? Usually sending it out of the Church to do childish activities! God has given us a key and we are dismissing it!

Secondly, it is very difficult for adults to evangelise in any specific geographical area. Ask the Jehovah's Witnesses how many converts their approach wins for them. However, think about your children. One child has immediate access to one whole family. If God chose to give that one child a really powerful blessing, that child could affect his or her family in a more powerful way than any church representative could knocking on the door.

That child goes to school. That gives them immediate access to at least 25 other children of whom at least 20 are unlikely to be active Christians. If that one child could impart the blessing they had been given, at least half their class could be affected. That could lead to 10 families receiving a blessing. And so it goes on. I have heard people talk about power evangelism, but this 'snowball effect' could make this the most explosive form of evangelism the world has ever seen!

Is ministry to children important?

It is worth noting at this point that a recent survey showed that over 90 per cent of today's active adult Christians found their faith before the age of 21! These figures are quoted from the Office of Population, Censuses and Surveys.

Is it any wonder that teachers trying to introduce 'children's church' come under attack! Is it any wonder that some could buckle under the pressure!

The biggest problem is that you may have vision for your Sunday school class, but a move like this needs the blessing and support of the whole Church – especially the leadership team! If you do not have the support of the Minister it will be very difficult to have this type of Sunday school – as you will see later. Co-operation and team work are the by-words. Hence this book. If you can present a reasoned argument to your leadership team – then you have a chance of success. If you cannot present a solid case, then the introduction of this type of Sunday school teaching will probably fail – as it did with us on our first attempt.

People will have doubts, and people will say – 'Yes, we see your vision . . . but we are not ready yet – we will be one day – but not yet . . . and anyway we want to know *how!*'

Remember Peter? An experienced fisherman who had spent years living on the water. He knew the properties of water better than most. He stepped out of a boat into what he knew was totally and utterly impossible – but as long as his eyes were on Jesus he did the impossible!

This little book is not about the impossible. Neither is it a formula of success – but it does present you with possible strategies and reasons for at least trying to break the mould into which Sunday school teaching has been 'set' for generations. It will help you to break the traditional concrete into which our work with children has been encased.

But why bother? Why not stay in our old, set ways? The answer is simple. Children can achieve what we, as adults, can't! That sounds strange when we think of the educational system, and all the traditions of our society. But God knows children are important. He is already using them powerfully.

Some testimonies

An 8-year-old girl stood up in her church in Leicester in early May 1999 and gave a prophecy. The word she gave did not seem significant . . . until the minister admitted afterwards that he had prepared the sermon he felt God wanted him to give – only to reject it at the last minute as he knew it could upset someone he had seen sitting in the congregation . . . and then he had rapidly prepared a new address! However, the word given by the child spoke into the first sermon, so he braced himself and delivered the original sermon. The person he had been concerned about offending was so convicted by the sermon that they went forward at the end of the service for prayer and salvation! 'Out of the mouths of babes and sucklings . . .'

In *Spread the Fire*, issue 2, 1999 (this is the church magazine from Toronto Airport Christian Fellowship – TACF) there is a report written by a 13-year-old pupil about the revival that has hit her school at Folly's End, Croydon! One teacher felt certain that 'she felt the Holy Spirit say "This is my school, not yours!"' The writer, Jessie Markee, states, 'At some meetings we have heard angels singing and a lion roaring. God told us there was going to be an *uproar* in England and the rest of the world *with the youth*.' She also reports of miracles and to a significant healing. As a result of God's involvement at Folly's End, the church there (Folly's End Christian Centre) started 'children's church' in September 1999! Praise the Lord. I understand that this church is growing into a major oasis in that part of London, and Jessie's mother, Zee Markee, has a regular programme on the God channel.

Several healings have been reported in various schools in Leicestershire by a supply teacher who reported that, at the end of one day during which he had shared about the power of prayer, a child announced, 'It works, it works!' In response to the obvious question she reported that when her friend fell and hurt her wrist she had said a prayer for it and God had stopped it hurting . . . *immediately!* Praise the Lord!

Some stories quoted by Heather Thompson at Grapevine – August 1999:

> A 4-year-old boy (Tyler) suddenly started wanting to pray for up to *one hour* at night! As a result his nominally Christian family started to change dramatically!
>
> An 8-year-old girl spoke prophetically over adults she did not know and *correctly* reiterated prophecies and secret dreams they had been given months previously.
>
> A *3-year-old* girl suddenly started laying hands on the adults. *All* were deeply affected . . . by a 3-year-old!

Testimony given by an ex-Sikh at 'Christian Millennium Praise' in Victoria Park, Leicester, on Saturday, 10 June 2000: He was one of five Sikh children brought up in a strict Sikh family in Leicester . . . but one day his little sister went home from school having heard some stories during the day about Jesus, and decided as a result to become a Christian! Her ministry was so powerful that she not only ignored the taunts from the other siblings – she converted them *all* to Christianity as well!

Ely Christian Fellowship held a 'Son Seekers' summer club in August 2000. Five children from totally unchurched families asked for prayer and made a commitment to follow Christ. One, an 8-year-old boy – went home and immediately started trying to convert his family! Children can do what adults can't!

A recent survey in the United States showed that 85 per cent of Christians in America became Christians *between the ages of 4 and 14!*

One worship leader in Leicestershire has suddenly realised that children *are more sensitive to God's presence than he is!* As a result he has a small group of children worshipping on, or in front of the stage. If they are not 'responding' during the worship he accepts the fault as being his, and changes the direction in which he is leading. If they are responding well, he will select more hymns of the same type. He directs, but God is 'leading' the direction in which the worship is going – through his children!

Churches are currently spending quite large sums of money trying to save adults – which is highly commendable and must be encouraged – but how much money, support and genuine interest is being paid to the 4 to 14s? Yet less than 10 per cent of the adult Christian population are adult converts, because over 90 per cent of the Christian population is converted before they reach their fourteenth birthday!

Pastor Vann Lane tells us in his book that we must not go looking for new ways to *entertain* the children in Sunday school. That we must not go looking for new books with new or slightly different things presented in a slightly different way. He goes on to tell us that in his view children can easily be entertained and kept quiet with a string of interesting videos, sweets and bags of popcorn. However, every time we simply entertain the children, we are sacrificing the precious time we have with them. If we simply entertain the children we are *totally failing* to fulfil the commission God has given us!

A prophecy given by Jim Paul (TACF) at Dudley Grace Centre on 20 February 2000, included these words: 'The days for traditional Sunday school are over. *Sunday school is dead!* Children and young people will be very important in the work God is *now* about to do!'

If you feel challenged, but you want some ideas and thoughts – read on!

Where could we go next?

When we realised what God wanted us to do, rather like Peter in the days of Jesus, we leapt out of the boat and . . . expected everyone else to follow!

In the famous Bible story we usually focus on Peter, and the wavering of his faith. When he had faith, he walked on water. When he took his eyes off Jesus, he started to sink. Know the feeling? We are told about Peter's weakness in taking his eyes off Jesus and taught to keep our focus on the Lord. This is all very good, but what we often forget is that *all* the other disciples *stayed in the boat!* They didn't even *try* to follow Peter into his impossible situation! Even when Peter was right there, next to them, they still did not follow his example.

When people begin to realise what this vision is all about, a lot will want to get on board, but because the initial vision is not theirs, many will have all the practical questions that need to be answered before they feel that they can launch out into the unknown! Like the other disciples – the majority will sit and watch in awe – not daring to leave the security of the boat!

How do you start to do something new when everything you are doing has been done that way for years?

What direction should you take?

You could decide to launch into 'children's church' like Pastor Vann Lane in Pensacola. If this is the course of action you follow, then you must read his book, *Children of Revival.* This is the course he felt led to follow. His 'children's church' is very much like 'adult' church, except that it is organised by, and run by children. They have their own ministry time (as with adults) only it is trained children who minister to their peers. There have also been times when the children have been invited into the main church to minister to the adults.

When we started on the road of trying to enable our children to get closer to God, this was the direction we were also trying to go in. At that time we ran a large youth group and a small Sunday school, and we saw the youth group as the 'outreach' wing of our ministry, and the Sunday school as the growth and development wing. We wanted to take the Sunday school children out of traditional church from the moment they arrived, and run a parallel 'children's church' most Sundays. This, however, would have a knock-on effect on the main service as it would have involved a total restructuring of the entire church service programme as well! Out would have gone the traditional format, the children's address (story time), and the children's performance spots at Mother's Day, etc.

It's very easy to see the changes you may want to introduce to 'Sunday school' without allowing for the effect those changes will enforce on the main meeting. Even the terms I am using in this section devalue the importance of children. One gets into the mindset of seeing the adult meeting as 'the main meeting', and the children's meeting as something stuck on at the side to keep the children out of the way whilst the adults do 'real God'! But remember – 90 per cent of all adult Christians were converted before their fourteenth birthday! So really, the adult meeting is generally only just looking after the established converts. The *real* meeting is where the children are; where the real outreach is taking place; where the wheels of evangelism hit the road! But have you tried to sell this concept to a typical, traditional church? You can begin to see the problem! Children's church is not just taking a new approach to teaching a few kids in Sunday school, it's also taking a new approach to the whole concept of 'church'! It's also teaching the adults the importance of their children – *not* when they've grown up and become adults – *but now!*

So is children's church the only answer? We used to think so, but once you start looking at the importance of children, then you can see the problem from a different perspective.

When we read the Bible, we often apply *our* logic to certain passages without thinking of the full implications. In the feeding of the 5000, Mark records that the loaves and fish fed 5000 men! (Mark 6:44). Does that mean that there were no women and children present? Or perhaps that the food was only given to the men? Obviously not! There had to be at least one small boy present! But in the culture of the time families were often counted by the head of the family – the men. This we accept as being quite obvious, but how often do we exclude children when in gospel times they would have been included automatically.

The Bible is full of expressions like 'all', 'everyone' and 'the whole nation'. This obviously *includes* the children. If you look at the well-known story of Paul and Silas in prison (Acts 16:30-34), Paul and Silas told the jailer: 'You will be saved – you *and your household.*' That phrase includes children, servants and relatives staying in the house at that time. The jailer then became a believer, and 'he and *all his family* were baptised'. He was also very happy because 'he and *his whole family*' had become believers!

What does Jesus say about children? This is even more challenging. For example:

> At that time Jesus said, 'I praise you, Father, Lord of heaven and earth, because you have hidden these things from the wise and learned, and revealed them *to little children.*' (Matthew 11:25, NIV)

You can't be much more direct than that, can you! Although, through inclusive words such as 'all his family' children are generally included throughout the Bible, there are occasions when adults are apparently excluded by Jesus!

Who do you want as a teacher?

If I want to improve my skills at playing cricket I find a good player or coach. I don't go looking for a golf pro! If I want to go scuba-diving I have real problems! I certainly won't stop the first fisherman I see and ask for his help. I won't even ask my best and most trusted friend – who just happens to be a first-class mountaineer! I know that my life is at risk in the water. If I am to learn in safety I want a well-trained, experienced scuba-diver to teach me. This may all seem very obvious. But think carefully about the lesson here. If I want to improve my chances of doing something – especially something dangerous – then I will find someone who is much better qualified than me.

So here's the key question! Is your soul safe? Do you want to go to heaven? If you do, then you should find someone who can help you. Someone who has a *better chance* of getting there than you do. Someone who can show you the way. Someone better qualified than you are. Who should you consider? Perhaps some highly ranked bishop? A highly respected minister? A mature adult who is also a mature Christian? I am certain that all these people could offer you some helpful advice. Some of that advice may be brilliant, and some not quite so helpful. But what advice did Jesus give us?

Now here's the humbling bit! He said, 'I tell you the truth'. This is a phrase Jesus sometimes used when he wanted to give his words even more importance than usual. So the fact he starts off in this way means that the next few words are highly significant! 'I tell you the truth, unless you change and become like *little* children you will *never* enter the kingdom of heaven' (Matthew 18:3, NIV). Note the word 'never'. This is not a grey area. There are no 'perhapses' in his statement. 'Unless you become like *little children.'* He does not even say nice, mature teenagers! He specifically says 'little children'. 'Unless you become like little children you will *Never* . . . '! One little word can carry such infinite and final power can't it! So here comes the difficult bit. If you have accepted my arguments regarding swimming and diving, then you have to accept the same arguments regarding our spiritual acceptance of God. If you want to enter heaven, you need to be with, so that you can learn from . . . little children!

This brings us back to 'children's church'. If children are the key for your entry into heaven, do you want to send them out of 'adult' church every week?

I know there will be a whole lot of objections to children staying in church. The young mum who looks forward to her time of worship, but she can't as long as little Timmy is hanging on to her leg crying! Or what do you do if little Jenny needs her milk? Yes, there are a few practical problems, so before we look at what the children can give to us adults, let's look at some of the problems.

Tiny babies can suddenly have a need for a feed! If it is possible, try to provide a little comfortable area at the back of the church where a mum can take her child for feeding, this allows her to still feel part of the service without feeling embarrassed at having to feed, especially if she is breastfeeding. I know of some churches that have sectioned off a small area with soundproof glass. This allows the service to be transmitted into the enclosed area without any sound escaping from it. Mums (or dads) can then return with their child as soon as they have become settled, and they can see it is a convenient time to return.

My secret weapon in these situations was two slices of hard toast spread with Marmite. My boys loved it, and two slices was just enough to get through a whole service. The only problem I had with this method was that other young children always ended up sitting close by so that they could share the supply, so four slices became a more realistic quantity to take!

The church is supposed to be a *family*. In my family, my children were often passed around from person to person. Sometimes one person could have a better influence on the child than another. Why not in church? A mum – especially if she is a single parent – must get desperate for the chance to forget everything for a few moments and just worship God. Provided the child is willing to go to another person, it is not a major sacrifice to give up part of your worship so that the mum can have a few moments of worship herself. If done on a regular basis, the child would soon get used to a number of different surrogate parents helping 'Mum' on a Sunday morning, and Mum would be able to look forward to her church visits as she would know that help was always at hand. What mums usually get is a condemning stare as if it is their fault that the child has or is a problem! Condemnation or blessing? Remember, these children are the keys to the kingdom! How will this affect your attitude to young children in church?

Dealing with boredom

'But my child can't sit still!' Some children do have difficulty sitting down or keeping still for more than two minutes. I know! I've got three very active boys! We have taken small soft toys, toy cars, colourings and anything else we could think of to try to contain our children. But what are the children telling us? Usually, with an older child, much of the unsettled behaviour is because they are bored! Whose fault is that? Usually not the child's! Children are not miniature adults. Most of them cannot sit still for more than five minutes. Most of them cannot focus on an adult talking for more than five minutes. Indeed, many adults struggle in this area but they have just learned to hide their feelings better! Yet we expect the children to be quiet, to rise and sit at all the correct places, and to sit through an address or sermon which many adults often find as inspiring as a fish shop menu!

So keeping children in church does not result in a problem free service! Far from it! Hence the reason why a number of churches have gone along the road of 'children's church'. So what is children's church? Surely it must be just Sunday school with a new name?

Sunday school by another name?

No! Children's church is a totally different concept. There are many reasons why children's church may be the best answer for a church to consider.

Having recently attended a historic little country church that had been beautifully preserved as a 'listed' ancient monument, I am aware of the restrictions that buildings can impose on your activities. We were moving along the road towards children's church, and in that situation I think it was possibly the best answer. A number of the congregation were still struggling to accept the use of a piano and keyboard instead of the somewhat mothballed organ, so to have suggested holding the meetings in the more child-friendly environment offered by the hall next door would have been a very difficult decision. And the concept of organising a child-friendly service cramped into highly polished and uncomfortable pews would have been bordering on the ridiculous! However, we do feel that in this current move of God, which is bringing a direct focus onto the children – no matter what the difficulties are, every possible effort should be made to involve, accept and learn from the children. If we do this, we will be living our Christian lives in line with Jesus' teaching on children and their direct importance in our own salvation. We will also be doing – or being 'church' in the same way that the early Christians were.

The activities used in children's church can be the same as those followed by the adults. Children can enjoy worshipping God in just the same way that adults do – except that in a child's culture, pipe organs do not play a part any more than Gregorian chants or the majority of hymns written over 100 years ago do!

God can use his children to minister to others – just as he can use adults. Sometimes the results are even better when children pray because children are not limited by their own logic and understanding. They do not approach prayer ministry carrying in their own baggage as some adults do.

They can even enjoy an address or sermon – provided that it is directed at their level! This does not mean that it should be 'childish'. That is one of the biggest mistakes adults make when planning for children. Hymns and stories are often chosen and presented as if the recipients are only 3 years old! More on all this later!

Often children's church is a misunderstood concept, whereby parents can deliver their children to the children's section before going on to the 'main' or adult service. The children cannot cause any problems to them as they are 'out of the way'! Unfortunately, if you look back at Matthew 18:3 you will realise that what is happening is that our 'teachers', who should be helping us into the kingdom through their example, have been left outside the adult meeting. The 'main' meeting is, in reality, now being held next door in the children's section! A challenging thought! Could the children get straight into the kingdom and leave us behind?

However, as I have already observed, there will be some situations in which, for a whole variety of reasons, children's church is the only option available to a specific church group.

The children's church option

If, as a fellowship, you decide to go along the 'children's church' path, then you can't just change the name of the Sunday school but otherwise carry on as before. There will be a number of decisions that have to be made.

I would suggest that you write out a complete plan of a typical service as a starting point, then you do a plan of an 'ideal children's church' as you see it. Put both plans beside each other and look at the changes that are involved. There are some questions near the end of this book that will help you to make the decisions necessary.

Traditional Sunday school usually seems to require the children to leave the service just prior to the address. The children then need to be entertained (or taught) for about the length of an average sermon.

The teaching usually follows a plan as set out in one of the general series of Sunday school books, and involves listening to a Bible story, some small activity and a colouring.

Sadly, Sunday school teaching has often been relegated to being an 'also ran' when church duties are allocated. It is far more 'important' to be in the choir or the worship team than teach little kids in another building. This devaluing of the importance of teaching the children can result in people leading the Sunday school on a rota – because they don't want to 'miss out' on what's happening next door every week! The 'book' and the set programme become the only continuity from week to week, and slowly the programme book becomes the cage from which there seems to be no escape!

If you think your Sunday school teachers may have fallen into this rut, you may decide to try to keep 'everyone on board' by phasing in some of the other activities. This can work, especially if you have a key worker who can instigate the changes almost alone. However, the best way to introduce radical changes is to make all the decisions necessary and go for it, totally committed from the start. Otherwise some people who still hanker for the 'old cage' will do enough – not deliberately

– to show that the changes are not working. When you have only partly 'phased in' the changes, it would be even easier to phase them out again!

The four Ws approach

So where should you be heading? Children's church should be very similar to the very best of 'adult' church. Children should be brought to the children's section before the start of the main meeting. Their meeting should be far less formal than a traditional adult meeting, but otherwise it should contain all the elements of a complete church service. As a frame, I personally like the principles of the four Ws approach. (This is the service frame as developed by the cell churches.) As children arrive there is something 'light' for them to be involved in. This is the 'Welcome' time, and it could involve any of the welcome or warm-up activities outlined later. From the welcome you can move the children into a place of Worship. Children enjoy modern hymns. There are some that are very 'active' such as 'Who paints the skies', or 'We want to see Jesus lifted high', but they are equally at home with the same modern intimate hymns and even the updated versions of the old faithful hymns that adults enjoy. Once you get established let the children suggest hymns that they would like to sing. There are some very talented teenagers around, and if you are fortunate enough to have some in your church try to encourage the development of a teenage worship group. Children have just as much of a right to have 'live' worship as adults. If live music cannot be provided, do not let this put you off! There are some very good tapes and CDs available. See the section on Worship (page 29) for more help with this topic. Some churches are already reorganising their service so that the main worship leader and key members of the worship team can be available for the children's time of worship.

The Word given to children can be just as powerful and challenging as the word given to adults, but remember the age of the children. They will not sit still through a 30-minute dry talk about God's view on their behaviour! If God wants to tell them what *he* thinks, let him! Otherwise the children's address should be short, direct, interesting – and obviously Bible-based.

The final W is the Witness aspect. Most services for adults don't include this, and yet the last words we have recorded as having been spoken by Jesus are those often referred to as 'The Great Commission' – go into the world and tell, and yet most adults leaving church will dwell briefly on the service and return quickly to 'normal' life! Children, however, will accept Jesus' request, and will go into the world telling other children about Jesus. All they need is a level of accountability and some encouragement. Hence the need for a witness section.

I could write a lot more about 'children's church', but I suggest that if this is the direction you decide to take, then *Children of Revival* is essential reading. Pastor Lane had a fairly conventional 'Sunday school', and, like all Sunday school leaders, was always looking for helpers. Then he changed his approach and started children's church. Once children's church was up and running a strange thing happened. He found there were more people wanting to help with the children than he wanted. He was placed in the wonderful position of being able to select which workers he wanted from a waiting list! Why? Because as soon as God was allowed into the situation, the children started to grow! They reached the point where they were not just taking from, and draining the adult helpers, but were also able to contribute towards the spiritual growth of those adults – often in a more profound way than would have happened had they stayed in the main service. The result? A waiting list of adults wanting to help!

The IG service

So what about 'all age' or 'family' worship? Aren't they different names for the same thing? No, not really true, although 'all age' worship seems to have become a name sometimes used for a family service where there is an attempt to sound more up to date!

In most of the churches I have been to, family worship has been the name given to the service in which the children are present – possibly because the usual teachers are on holiday – or because they have a 'performance' they have been practising that they want to show everyone. In these services the sermon is often reduced to two or three bite-sized chunks to make it more 'child friendly', even if it is still way above their heads. Occasionally the members of one family will be involved in doing something – to give the service a 'family' feel.

All-age worship, however, should mean that the full age range present can be involved in the service, and that the entire service can be understood and entered into by almost everyone present except for *very* young children.

In a full 'family church', there will be people who can help struggling mums with their children. For the worship, there should be ways of involving the children – perhaps through the provision of flags they can wave, or space where they can express themselves through dance.

An IG service is possibly a better name for this type of service as it avoids confusion. IG stands for Intergenerational – so it is planned with all generations in mind.

In the early 1990s I read *Church in the Market Place*, in which George Carey describes how he felt when a young lady offered her services to help with the worship . . . as a dancer! As I read I wondered what he would do. To my surprise he hesitated and then invited her to dance! In those days I don't think I would have been so open. Then I saw some Korean dancers helping with the worship at Spring Harvest. They were brilliant and they really enhanced the worship.

I had a very 'traditional' upbringing, and, as a young man, the only dancing I considered acceptable was ballroom dancing. I have had to change a whole lot of my traditional 'values' in recent years. But then, if King David could be so caught up in worship that half his clothes fell off when he danced before the ark, we should be able to get fully involved in our worship as well, and who better to lead us than the children!

If you finally decide to keep your children *in* church as the general rule then what do you do with them? How can you learn from them? Where should you hold your meetings? Is it possible to 'prepare' your children for life in the main meeting?

Clearly, just to carry on as you are, but to make the children stay *in* the main meeting is a recipe for disaster! Is it possible to prepare your children for their role of teaching the adults?

'Training' children

In the old 'Sunday school', the adult leaders were the 'teachers' and the children, rather like in conventional school, were the subjects to whom the teachers delivered their messages. The teachers did all the 'giving', and the children were expected to be little sponges, absorbing all the wisdom given by the teachers.

In this new situation, the adult leaders are 'facilitators' rather than teachers. Their job is to create situations in which the children are encouraged to grow. It's a bit like gardening. When seeds are beginning to grow a gardener doesn't stand talking to them telling them what to do. He provides them with a good growing environment. He provides adequate water, heat and light – and after due passage of time he should have a nice healthy plant.

As a very poor gardener, I have occasionally looked at a gardening book to try to help me improve my skills in certain areas, and to develop skills in areas in which I was almost clueless!

The purpose of the next few sections is rather like a gardening manual. Your 'soil' may be different from mine, but there are certain basic concepts that work no matter what your soil is like.

With gardening, it's not just the plants that need developing and nurturing; the gardeners also need help and updating! I have been involved in youth work for over 40 years, and have always been able to draw children into youth groups. When my wife and I were invited to get involved in the youth work in our present church, I anticipated an immediate big rise in the attendance figures. But God had other ideas! Our numbers have grown, but the most noticeable change that has occurred is that instead of the club 'getting fat' with numbers, the children have all grown spiritually.

God gave my wife and I a dream. Our children are already working in the prophetic. God is taking us through the prophecy of Joel (Acts 2:17 and Joel 2:28). This is end times!

We are taking our children through a number of steps. Some of these steps are fairly short, others take some time. How long each step takes you will depend very much on you, your children . . . and God! Our plans will only get in the way if God has other plans for you and your group, so the first important lesson is to be open to what God is telling you. So listen to God! And remember – you should be leading by example, so you do need to follow these steps before the children start their 'training', and with the children.

Listen to God

If you carefully follow a recipe in a cookery book, you *will* get good results. This book is *not* a recipe book. You must always put God above all else, be open to what he is telling you, and go with it.

Worship

We spent a long time working on our worship. We have tried various approaches, and when we have tried to go into worship for the sake of worship, we have always had success. Our children have really grown in their relationship with God, and some of them are already in a place where they can lead us!

Asking God questions

This can give children tremendous encouragement. They can discover that God is real, talks to them . . . and loves them! That is the big one!

Seeking God's word for others

We often ask God questions, and expect answers! Already this has resulted in one of our senior pastors taking six young people to India on a missionary journey. Why did she go? Because God told her to through a 9-year-old girl!

Asking God's guidance

Asking God's guidance on issues that affect the children personally has been very rewarding and encouraging for the children.

Setting a scene

The leader sets a scene in which Jesus talks to the children. Again, this can be very rewarding both for the children and the leaders.

Talking in tongues

This was the next step we were given. However, I am aware that some churches do interpret Paul's teaching in Corinthians in different ways. But certainly for us, this had to be the next step.

Teaching why
All this must have a purpose. We may not see it, and it may just look like 'another programme', but it isn't! This is leading the children to the point at which they can start to fulfil the requirement of the great commission.

Rewards and riches
God makes a number of prophetic statements in the Bible, many of which we often tend to 'overlook' in our ministry. But they are promises, and as God is true to his word, the children can expect to receive something for following Jesus' instructions.

How to become a warrior
Having been prepared with everything God has available to us, the final stage is preparing the children to go out into the world . . . and to win it for Christ!

Other little steps
In the time between this book being accepted for publication and the drafts being completed, God has shown us a few more little 'stepping stones'. Details will be included of these, but they will be brief, as the 'little steps' he has for you may well be different from the little steps he has given us.

Putting on the glaze
This programme is like making a pot. When the pot has been completed – to human eyes – it would be easy to say, 'Well, that's it! Now where do we go?' An unglazed pot is not always waterproof, and it doesn't look its best! So your completed pot will need glazing!

This is an exciting programme, and with God's blessing and guidance, it will end Sunday school as we have known it!

The start of this programme must include a basic teaching on listening to God and to worship; and the end of the programme should include the teaching of 'why' the children are being empowered and armed for battle! The order in which the middle steps should be taken depends on how God guides you! See the section on 'Other little steps', page 43.

The stepping stones

Listening to God

In recent years a number of key people in the body of the Church have been given a prophetic 'vision' or insight into the world situation. If you read Christian magazines, or watch Christian television programmes, you will have noticed that quite suddenly a lot of people from totally different backgrounds are all talking about the way God is moving at the moment. We are seeing a number of significant healings in different parts of the world. There seem to be a lot of people who all believe we are very near to the 'end times' Jesus talked about. In the past there have been small groups who have had these 'thoughts', but not in the significant numbers we are getting today. I can remember when I was taking one of my O-level examinations at the end of the 1950s, the teacher invigilating told as that as the world was due to end part-way through the exam none of us might be there at the end, but he wished us 'good luck' anyway! This 'prophecy' – quite apart from the fact that its very nature was unscriptural, was taken as a joke by almost everyone! The prophecies of today are different.

I believe we are very much into 'end times'. Because of that, I believe that God is about to 'turn up the heat', and if you are truly listening to his promptings, that could send you in a totally different and new direction. If you follow this guide, be always aware that God may start to 'do a new thing', and if you are not listening, you will not know what he wants you to do!

'Leading' children in these last days is a very challenging and responsible task. Some will succeed and some will fail. But remember, you are God's 'human hands' in preparing his final army! Now that's awesome!

Worship

For us, this has been a vital and essential starting point. The Bible tells us that God inhabits the praise of his people, so what better place could there be to start!

During the worship, children seem to stay with their parents – often because the seating makes movement very difficult unless you are prepared to put up with the judgemental looks you will get as your dainty, light-footed angel stamps on Mrs Brown's feet yet again! Rather than subject yourself to *the stare* you order him or her to be quiet and keep still! And what are you doing? Probably standing up, possibly clapping in time with the hymn, or even raising your arms in the air. Meanwhile your little angel has to 'keep still'. This would seem to be rather unrealistic.

Many churches do not have the restriction of pews, but this freedom can bring its own problems, because as soon as the children may leave their seats, some will just wander aimlessly around. Sometimes chasing after some long lost friend that they haven't seen for at least two minutes, or grabbing a flag so that they can emulate the success of the three musketeers with their erstwhile friend. Not quite the sword of 'truth' that Paul had in mind – but there you are! That's kids for you! So how can you move them from being junior tearaways into being worshippers?

When I was a boy I liked to play with a toy car. It was a very special car to me as it had proper steering, so I could play (practise) steering in and out between objects. I even tied a trailer on the back so that I could reverse between objects. This was a very good learning process. It was not a real car. I could crash into the books as often as I liked, and no one ever got hurt. No one ever laughed at me for playing with a car that was not real. We all accept these standards for play, and yet some eyebrows will go up in horror at the thought of 'playing church'. But what better way is there to learn? Children play shops; doctors and nurses, and the one that should really alarm us all – mums and dads! But we don't worry about the babies!

So – we start by playing at worship! What we have done is to carefully select four or five worship hymns. Each hymn should be different from the others, so one might be a really 'boppy' modern children's hymn such as 'Who paints the skies'. The words are projected onto the wall through an OHP so that the children have a clear view of them. This particular hymn has a lot of actions, so it's quite fun for the children to do. But remember, children learn by copying! So you can't just let them loose and expect them to 'get on with it'! You have to get on with it in front of them!

This may sound very challenging, but as I said earlier, the rigid steps of classic ballroom dancing (only bronze level) was my limit. But to quote from a 60s hit – 'If my friends could see me now!' More to the point, if they could see my shy, reserved wife – out in the front with the children! But that really is what this is all about. The children need a role model – and if you are a children's leader, that means you! . . . But you can get help!

We found a retired PE teacher who had taught dance, and she came in to lead a few sessions. We learned as much from her as the children did, and she equipped us to go much further. As she was a very active Christian, she could use her skills in genuine worship, and have the children copy her movements. Then, as the children got used to the idea, she developed the movements further. We then asked the children if any of them would like to lead for a few moments. We only needed a few volunteers which we quickly got, and she would suddenly say, 'Don't watch me, follow Abbie.' Abbie would lead for twenty seconds or so, then another name would be called. This progressed to the point where we could start telling the children to copy anyone – adult or child – or simply do their own thing.

We then used a similar approach with a second or third hymn. As a general rule we would not use more than two or three hymns in any one session. Then we could get the children to focus on the words, what they meant, and to interpret them through their dance.

At first the children were 'playing'. They were copying who ever was leading and following their actions rather than worshipping God. However, it was only a matter of weeks before some of the children began to emerge as real worshippers. They now dance and wave flags in the main celebration, and their actions have inspired the adults to start getting involved.

At first the children would only use dance in worship if one of the leaders made the first move. However, within a very short time some of the children reached that place where they genuinely wanted to worship themselves – even when standing alone with no one else there either to lead them or to encourage them. We have some who carry such a blessing in their worship that they can lift everyone else simply by starting their own, personal worship of God. This immediately elevates their 'dance' from a performance to one of 'leading worship' and encouraging others to worship in true freedom. Now isn't that what worship leading is really all about?

The children can worship through quiet dance, 'boyish' dance with large, physical movements, or flags – which we have shown don't have to be waved all the time. They can be put down and moved around before being picked up again. Even when your children have reached the point at which they can worship through dance without any input from you, remember that worship has a vital role in our communications with God, and should therefore play an active part in all our meetings – with or without children!

Any budding DJs?

Worship can be led very well using tapes and CDs, but there is nothing like live worship! A live worship leader may never get remotely close to the quality of a recorded hymn, but if they are sensitive to the Holy Spirit, and the way he is working through the children, then they can quicken up, slow down, repeat a section of a hymn several times, or even suddenly go into a totally different hymn that fits in better with what God is doing. If possible, involve children in the worship leading. There are some very talented young people around these days, and they will possibly be more into whatever worship group is currently 'in' for young people than you are, groups such as Delirious?, Matt Redman, or Martin Smith.

If you have to rely on tapes and CDs, try to be well planned so that there are virtually no delays between hymns. This may mean re-recording a track that you want onto a tape so that you can perhaps play a CD, move straight to the tape, and have the next CD in place and ready to go before the tape finishes. If children are presented with long pauses interspersed with apologies and notes from the wrong hymn, they will very quickly lose their focus, and then you have lost them! This could be a training ground for young, potential DJs! We often record all the hymns we feel led to use onto one audio tape so that we can start off and just let the tape run. This is an excellent method – until you want to play a particular hymn a second time – and it isn't the first one on the tape! A tape recorder with a 'counter' is a great help.

Manipulate or facilitate?

Some people could say that we had manipulated the situation when we started to 'teach' the children to worship, but my answer to that is very simple. I see the developing role of children's leaders as being one of facilitation rather than of teaching. If you teach, you expect the children to copy exactly and to learn the steps and movements. In other words, to learn a performance. What we have done is to start off as if we were looking at a performance, but move very quickly into individual work. Initially we have facilitated the children's development of dance skills, but we have also created the opportunity for God to step in – and he often does! The children can then continue to grow in their worship without our help. They will overtake us. That is already happening here. I often follow one of the children in worship when I'm looking for the right movement to express what I want to show God. We have one boy in our group who almost objected to joining in the worship at first. He was very reluctant, and obliged very slowly. He recently reduced a member of the worship team to tears by his quiet and extremely expressive worship in a main service! We have a few girls who have taken off in their worship – but expressive dance is very much a natural way of expression for girls. When a boy can reduce members of the worship team to tears, and another 9-year-old boy can reduce a visiting minister to tears – then you know that the lessons were worth learning and have been learned.

In his book, *The Call*, Rick Joyner discloses some of the revelations he has been given. When we really worship God, it really makes him happy – especially those people who have 'cracked notes' as they can only be singing for God. I trust that God feels the same way about dance and worship!

Asking God questions

If children are to develop a relationship with God, then they must learn to talk to him – and listen for his answers. This is a skill or gift many adults never develop, but you will be surprised just how quickly children will learn to work in this area.

A good starting point is to talk about the meaning of the cross – that Christ died for us – because he loves us that much! Then get the children to close their eyes and imagine seeing Jesus standing in front of the cross. Ask them to say in their minds, 'Do you really love me that much?' As they get an answer they should raise a hand and seek your acknowledgement. You should then either go to them and write down the reply they got, or with older children, give them a piece of paper and ask them to write down what God said to them. You will be surprised how many get an answer very, very quickly! When they have an answer, ask them to think of the person they like best. It can be a parent, but it doesn't have to be. Tell them to ask Jesus how much he loves their chosen person. (Be careful how you word this.) Then ask them to think about someone they don't like very much. Ask Jesus the same question.

This may seem a very simple, and almost engineered starting point, but would you expect to start driving for the very first time in the middle lane of a 7-lane freeway in America? Obviously not! My father started teaching me to drive on a deserted winter beach. How unreal was that! But it allowed me to learn the controls before I was expected to cope with the real road, and real traffic!

Whatever the children say should, if possible, be written down and kept. This may become important later.

> 'I'm too skinny!' (8-year-old Esther)
> 'You're my princess!' God's answer. What an encouragement!

On a subsequent occasion you can make a similar start, but then ask them to ask Jesus if he has any 'words' for them, or any plans for their lives. You may well be surprised at the level of maturity the children show in this.

> 'I will love you, even if you don't love me. I will love you wherever you are. God and I both love you. I am Jesus and I love you and will not hurt you. I am Jesus – King of kings.' (10-year-old Karl)

You can move on to words for other people. The leadership of the church is a good starting point. 'Would you like to ask Jesus if there is something he would like to say to the minister?' – or anyone else they see as being in the leadership of the church. You could ask them to write down the names of those people they see as being in the 'leadership' team, and to select one to pray about. Get them to ask God what he would like to say to them. (Don't judge the names of the people they give you. Children will often perceive someone else's position in the church in a different way than we do.)

The next phase could be asking Jesus what he thinks of certain issues that have been in the news, or that you have been discussing.

Seeking God's word for others

Sometimes we feel that God wants us to ask the children for a word either for specific church leaders or for visitors. We also use the church leadership as part of our 'training the children' programme.

The first time, we asked the children for a word for other people. We specifically asked for a word for the senior pastor. Knowing that we were doing a training exercise, he would have the maturity to either accept or dismiss these words.

We then asked the children to lie down, close their eyes and ask God for a word for the minister whilst we played quiet music. When they felt God had spoken we asked them to raise a hand. We then wrote down what they said. The words were passed on to the minister for his consideration. Some of the words given turned out to be quite prophetic!

Now we have confidence in God and our children, so when visitors come to visit the church, the children almost expect us to ask them for a word from God for them. Visitors have been reduced to tears on several occasions by the prophecies and words of encouragement God has given these people through our children.

Always start off by asking the children to ask for a word for someone who knows what you are doing. The minister or pastor are ideal people. Afterwards, quietly seek their reaction to the words given. This will give you an indication of how much the children are hearing from God.

If you are not sure how much the children are hearing, ask them for a word for someone else – perhaps even yourself. As soon as you find they are listening to God, and they are hearing what God has to say – let them loose on visitors. But remember, God will not usually speak through all the children, or even through the same children on more than one occasion.

It is very easy to label a child as being prophetic or not prophetic as the case may be, only to find the roles totally reversed on the next occasion. God will not respect your interpretation on his giftings to his children!

One also has to exercise wisdom on occasions, such as when given words which seem to contradict each other. From experience this is extremely rare. When God knows this could happen he usually gives a number of children a very similar word, which makes it quite easy to treat with caution the one conflicting word. But again, use caution as there have been occasions – especially in the Old Testament – when the anointed prophet has given a 'word' which is in direct opposition to the other prophets!

Asking God's guidance

This is an area that needs to be handled with care. Rather like the lovesick maiden who seeks God's guidance on the choice of a husband with the prayer, 'Lord, let it be the first man who knocks on my door tomorrow!'

Some teaching will be needed here on the appropriateness of the question being asked, although usually children are far better at seeking God's guidance than adults are!

Tell the children that they are going to have the chance to ask God for help or advice in any area. Then they, or a leader, should write down the question the child wishes to ask.

Then ask the children to lie on their backs, hands on their tummies whilst you play some suitable music – such as guitar praise, etc.

This can be a very good opportunity to use 'setting the scene' principles. Let the children see themselves lying in a field, looking up at the sky. A possible script follows:

'You are lying on the ground enjoying the hot sunshine as it warms your body and face. As you lie there thinking about your question, you hear a rustling sound. Someone is coming, but you feel very happy about it. The person stops beside you and you open your eyes and look up and see Jesus smiling down at you. He sits down on the grass next to you. You can see his love flowing out of his eyes towards you.

"I believe you want to ask me a question," he says. You can now ask your question, and listen carefully to the answer. When you have his answer raise your hand.'

At that point, depending on the age and ability of your children, they can either write down the answer God gave them, or a leader can go to them and write down the answer.

This is the time when you may need care and tact – although you may be surprised at the answers the children get to some of the most frighteningly real questions.

You should always respect a child's request not to show you their question or answer, but you should avail yourself to any child who wants to talk about either the question, or the answer they have been given.

Backs or tummies?

In most of these sessions we have the children lying on their backs. In this position, if they open their eyes they will only see the ceiling. If they lie on their tummies they will not feel so vulnerable, but boys will find it far easier to be distracted by some other child they can see. It is also far more difficult for them to imagine looking *up* to see Jesus if they are looking *down* towards the floor.

Setting a scene

The final directed level is to ask the children to lie or sit down, close their eyes and see a picture. This can be a picture that is totally from their own minds, or it may be one you direct. I have done this, and suddenly found that God has wanted me to 'change' the picture. Once you have set the scene, you ask them to imagine Jesus entering the scene. Whoever leads this exercise *must* be sensitive to the promptings of the Spirit, so that they will change the picture if so prompted.

In all these situations there will be some child or the other who doesn't get anything! If this happens encourage them to think of what Jesus *might* have said to them if he had spoken. Often God will be able to speak to them in this way. Again, everything that the children say can be written down. Some of the things they say may seem totally from 'them'. Don't worry. If a lot of the children are getting words, some children will make anything up so that they don't get left out. Don't ever condemn this. Write it down the same as you would for anyone else. I have seen children make up statements for several weeks, then suddenly come out with something so profound that it could only have come from God!

When Daphne Kirk, one of our senior leaders, was in America on a ministry tour, the children in her church in England were asked if they had a word for her. All the words given were e-mailed to her – including one quite strange one that God wanted to send her some flowers! Unbeknown to us, she had been fighting sickness during the tour. As she was sitting in her hotel room checking her e-mails she received our communication and, as she had already received some flowers, she thought that these were the ones referred to. However, before she could do anything else the doorbell rang. She opened the door to be greeted by the bellboy with a bunch of flowers someone had suddenly felt the need to send!

During a later tour of Indonesia, Daphne spent some time considering the various invitations she had to visit a number of different countries. Some offered just accommodation in homes, some offered good hotel accommodation, some offered full flights and accommodation. One could say an easy choice! But Daphne felt drawn to some of the poorer countries that were offering less – but which one? When she arrived home one of our most prophetic children greeted her with the words, 'God wants you to go to India!' So that was that! Within three months she was off again on one of the most challenging but most rewarding trips she has ever undertaken. She even took six of our young people with her. They all raised the money they needed for the flights themselves, and all had a very powerful experience. All because one young child spoke up. Don't ever underrate what God can say or do through his children.

Talking in tongues

This next section is really for church groups that already move in the gift of tongues, or that want to. However, before looking at the practical aspects of developing this gift I think it is important that we consider some biblical teaching on this topic, as it may provide answers for those who have questions.

As a starting point I think it is important that we remember John 14:12, when Jesus told his disciples, '. . . anyone who has faith in me will do what I have been doing. He will do even greater things than these . . .' Note that there are no 'dates' given. He does not say 'whilst I am still with you', or even 'whilst you, my disciples, are still alive'. So this statement must be 'for all time'. A clear indication that the Bible did not end either with the ascension of Jesus, or with the completion of the book of Revelation. From reading the book of Acts it is obvious that speaking in tongues was one of the 'new gifts' Jesus sent *after* his ascension! So tongues has to be a 'post-Jesus' gift.

The next question has to be, 'Do I have to be baptised in water first?' In Acts 19:6 it says: 'When Paul placed his hands on them, the Holy Spirit came on them and they spoke in tongues and prophesied.' Paul writes a lot about the gifts of the Spirit, including the gift of tongues (1 Corinthians 12:7). 'I would like every one of you to speak in tongues . . .' (1 Corinthians 14:5). Note that this letter does not say every one of you men, any one of you adults, or even anyone of you alive now – but simply every one of *you!* If we accept Paul's teaching as being relevant to us today, then that should apply to this teaching as well.

It seems clear that being baptised and receiving the gift of the Holy Spirit is often marked by the gift of tongues. So if we go to Acts 16:33 we see that after being released from prison, Paul and Silas told the jailer about Jesus, then, 'At that hour of the night the jailer took them and washed their wounds; then immediately he and *all his family* were baptised' [italics mine]. Again, we see that 'all his family' were involved – not just the adults.

How about developing the gift of speaking in tongues?

As we all know, children will copy adults so if they never hear any adults speaking in tongues, your task may be a little more difficult. However, if you have received the gift of tongues, then use it quietly but openly when you are with the children. Through your example they will learn that this is a gift given to us by God to be used!

The following are some ideas that we have seen used effectively in the development of this gifting.

A possible starting point

If you can select some situation or someone who needs prayer, this can be a good starting point. We know that it is our duty to pray for our leaders, so if you present your children with the name of a leader from, perhaps, the United Nations – the chances are they won't have even heard of them. How can they pray for someone they have never even heard of? Use tongues! Try it and try to establish how many children already genuinely have the gift. If very few – or perhaps none have the gift – then ask them if they would like it. If the answer is yes, you are into decision time! I suggest you note the reaction and move onto a new topic unless you have fully prepared the 'ground' in advance.

Before you start praying for the children, you should clear your potential actions with the senior pastor, and as a general rule with the parents of the children. You could do this on a one-to-one basis, or you could have a parents' meeting for the parents of all the children. This gives them the opportunity to hear in general terms what you propose to do, and it avoids misunderstandings later.

Once you have permission to proceed, there are several approaches you can use.

First, pray for the children and ask God to give them all the gift of tongues, or to wake up the gift if it may have been resting dormant for some time.

Then, to take the focus off what they are saying, have five seconds of very loud praying in tongues, followed by five seconds of very quiet praying. You can achieve this either by calling out 'loud' or 'soft' as required, or you can tell them to listen to your voice and change volume when you do. This allows you to vary the volume and keep the children focused on the leader. Usually, by focusing on you, what you are saying and the volume – they will forget what they are doing and will just go ahead in tongues.

Another way is for a leader to stand at the front and to make a single monosyllabic sound which the children may copy. Again the volume and pitch can be varied and the children asked to copy both the sound and the noise! After a few seconds, use a different sound. Then link the two together. Add a third. The children will very quickly lose the exact sound you are making. This is where the discernment comes in.

As you wander around you need to develop 'an ear' for what is happening. When you feel the time is right you have a choice of at least two actions.

1. You can stop everything and give the children an emotionally moving prayer topic. Again, this gives all of you a focus. Then start again, very quickly moving up to at least three types of sound. You could then bring in some prayer in English for your chosen topic, but quickly move into tongues. It is important that the leader is serious in what they are doing. First of all this is good modelling for the children, and secondly, when the children realise the leader is not listening to them, they will be encouraged to go for it!
2. If it feels right, go straight into longer sentences of prayer or worship. If you have managed to lift the children to the right place, God will bless them, and they will take off.

If it doesn't happen

With both these methods you may get some children who admit quietly later that it didn't happen for them. When this happens, always encourage the children. Tell them that you know God would want them to have the gift, and they will get it. In fact, since they were prayed for they almost certainly have already received it, but their minds are so busy that they haven't relaxed, and therefore haven't allowed the unfamiliar words to flow!

Children will often feel embarrassed by either having, or not having the gift of tongues. Always be sensitive to their feelings, and only ever give them encouragement. The Bible reading that I have already referred to and which is just so important in all this is, 'Let the little children come to me, and do not hinder them . . .' (Luke 18:16) or, as it says in *The Message*, 'Don't get between them and me. These children are the kingdom's pride and joy.'

I referred earlier to a trip organised by Daphne Kirk to India. She took with her a few of our young people, and during the visit she asked the parents and children she was working with if they would like to receive the Holy Spirit. That is *all* she asked! She asked the parents to lay hands on their own children, whilst she and her young team laid hands on the parents and prayed for the children through the parents. The children suddenly started praying in tongues! This in a church group in which *no one* had previously even heard anyone praying in tongues! There had been no modelling, and no mention of the gift of tongues, but God, through his supreme grace, just gave them the gift! The parents started asking what it was the children were talking about!

Through all this, it is essential that you never lose sight of the fact that God is in charge, not you, not me, and certainly not this, or any other book!

Also remember that the highest authority over children is their parents. If you have the parents working with, and alongside their children – then God will respect this. However, often this is not possible. Parents feel inadequate and refuse to be involved, and occasionally the parents are not active Christians and they may choose to delegate you to take responsibility.

This whole programme is so exciting and challenging – but requires great responsibility. Those who encourage their children to walk this road will reap rich rewards – but they also carry a big burden of responsibility. All these issues need to be handled with total openness, with all our personal baggage left right outside.

Teaching

At last! Some traditional teaching? Yes, but it's not the traditional bit of Bible stories and cut-out pictures, I'm afraid!

This type of programme is for one purpose and one purpose alone. To prepare God's children today for the battles they *are* fighting today and *will be* fighting tomorrow. What we have to teach the children is not the simple stories, but the message behind them. The whole of the Bible is an expression of God's love for his people. All his people – not just you and me! What we have been leading towards is helping the children to be able to feel what is on God's heart, and then to do something about it!

The starting point has to be God's love for the lost. Ever since human life began there has been a battle going on for the souls of man. That battle is rapidly nearing its climax and its ultimate conclusion. Those who accept Jesus as their Saviour will face a glorious future in heaven. The future for those who don't is very clearly stated in God's word. (See Matthew 13:42 and 25:41. These both make it very clear that hell is real and very unpleasant!) As end times approach God is mobilising the biggest and most powerful force ever put together. The children! He could so easily intervene and force us to accept his way, but he gave us all free choice. He wants us to choose to worship him and follow his commands. So he is mobilising an army of peers able to reach those parts that other peers can't reach!

There are already institutions that do not allow the open display of Christianity, even in England – a country that professes to be Christian. There are schools that openly flout the law regarding even an occasional Christian assembly.

Teachers are also actively encouraged to display a 'multi-faith' approach to their work – especially in the teaching of Religious Education. Teachers are discouraged from expressing any biblical truths as such, and are supposed to include the phrase 'Christians believe that . . .' either before or after making any positively Christian statement. Supply teachers are not being employed in some schools because of their open Christian approach to their work (Christian persecution in Britain!). Even the basic time AD and BC are being dropped by educationalists. BC has now become BCE! No longer is it Before Christ, but Before Common Era! Even at nursery schools, teachers are expected to give equal status to *all* faiths, even if no other faith is represented on its registers.

However, I know of a quite poor secondary school in which a number of children got together and started a Bible-teaching class. Children have got to be in school. No matter how 'open' they are about their faith, no headteacher would dare to expel or suspend a child for being too openly Christian! Is it any wonder that God is choosing children when adults are failing so abysmally!

When John the Baptist began to question whether or not Jesus was the Messiah, his disciples were told to tell John what they saw. How the blind received their sight and the dead were raised. Jesus knew that the evidence of his power would convince John that he really was Jesus.

The same applies today. When children lay hands on the sick and they are healed, people will *have* to take notice. Many still will not believe – but they will *have* to take notice!

It is around these facts that the teaching must be. Teaching the children to hear God's voice so they know what is on his heart. When they know what is on his heart and they pray for it, Jesus will answer those prayers and we will start to see children healing the sick, and displaying all the other gifts of the Spirit.

Teach the children how important they are to the kingdom *now*. Not when they have grown up – but *now*. Their value is in the fact that they *are* children, not that they are going to be adults one day. They have to 'Go into the world and tell all creation. Whoever believes and is baptised will be saved, but whoever does not believe will be condemned . . .' (Mark 16:15). That is what we are preparing our children for. That is the challenge.

Rewards and riches

God has shown us that we should also teach them about the rewards for following his way. God knows the challenges children face today. He knows just how many smoke, or have tried drugs whilst still very young. I have worked with children who were introduced to drugs well before leaving the primary school. I also know of a number of sexually active children, some still in their very early teens. God knows the intense peer pressure good kids have to put up with. He knows that dangling a carrot of rewards when they die is not enough. God will be blessing his children in many ways. I have no idea what they will be. I can only pass on what God has shown my wife on this issue, and that simply is that there will be great rewards for them. Use any Bible passage you can to illustrate how God has looked after those people who have placed him first, going right back to Noah. Everyone else perished in the flood except Noah and his family! No adults who were alive when the children of Israel lived in Egypt were allowed into the Promised Land – except Joshua and Caleb! Joshua and Caleb not only saw both countries, *they led* Israel in!

How to become a warrior

Some years ago I spent two years teaching in Khartoum, and my walk to school across the desert took me past the army camp where the Sudanese army was in training. Much of the training I saw each morning was their training in unarmed combat, and to every action there seemed to be a specific and loud shout! It was interesting to see the commitment and conviction the soldiers had. Although my knowledge of Arabic was extremely limited and I had no idea what they were saying, the message those shouts gave to me was – don't mess with us! We're out to win!

There is a lesson in that for us at this time. The Scripture the children need to declare is Ephesians 6. This can be acted out, shouted out, prayed or sung. Words and music for a possible song are included at the end of this booklet.

Aggressive prayer can be verbal or accompanied by a drum, or sticks banging on the ground, or simply the stamping of feet. You – and the children – can be as loud as you like as you prepare for the battle.

This may sound a little dramatic, but children are dramatic all the time. We have tried very hard (and failed) to keep toy guns out of the hands of our growing boys. There is a 'fleshly' desire to fight in most boys, whether it's cowboys and Indians or a re-enactment of the latest *Star Wars* battle. We have tried discouraging any 'bang bangs', only to be told that 'It's not a gun, but a proton zapper!' In the end we gave up! This dramatic approach to the 'Spiritual Battle' is a dramatisation at their level. They are used to seeing Indians, Korgs, or whatever, hiding behind the sofa, so for them to be wearing God's armour and marching out into the battle is actually quite easy! Possibly a bit more embarrassing for us though! Acting through the songs included in this book (or similar ones) should help.

Other little steps

In a period of only three months God has added more 'little stepping stones' that he wants us to walk on. The steps he wants you to take could be the same as ours – but they could be radically different, so it is important that you don't just tell the children to listen to God. You must set the example and do so yourself!

Learning verses

If we are preparing our children for battle, then it is our duty to fully arm and equip our troops! For this, they must have the only one piece of aggressive equipment Paul quotes in Ephesians 6 – the Sword of the Spirit. This, according to Paul – is the word of God!

When we covered 'How to become a warrior' we were suddenly convicted for not fully arming our soldiers! Every week they now learn a Bible verse, carefully selected to help them in their prospective battles, or the new stepping stone we are working on!

The Rapture
A topic which conversation with the children led us into, and the urgency of the battle to avoid too many people being 'left behind'!

Judgement
We were surprised how many of our children had no concept of God's final judgement and 'The Lamb's Book of Life'. Again, a topic inspired by their questioning.

Repentance
Why it is important to keep a 'short account with God' (Revelation 21:27).

Effective evangelism
Looking at the spiritual gifts of healing, miraculous powers and words of knowledge. How Jesus used them especially to convince John the Baptist who he was; with child-to-child ministry time for them to seek a prophecy for each other. On going through this process children may ask to be baptised. The Bible makes no distinction bewteen adults and children on this matter, but a useful guide to help you through the process of what baptism means is *When a Child Asks To Be Baptised,* by Daphne Kirk, published by Kevin Mayhew.

Putting on the glaze

In a prayer meeting Jackie was shown that we had effectively 'completed making a pot', and the children were now going through the firing process! Praise the Lord!

However, if you know anything about pottery you will know that a 'rough pot', even after firing, can still leak slightly, and it certainly doesn't *look* finished!

What we believe God wants us to do now is to take our pots – the children – and keep dipping them into the glaze – the stepping stones – until God decrees that they are 'ready for action'!

This will involve lots of worship, prayer, listening to God, seeking his will . . . and patience! (Something I lack!) As soon as the time is right *he* will fire the children. We certainly can't! Then they will become the cutting edge of the end-times army! Isn't that a challenging thought?

The battle plan

Although I have dealt with the steps you may have to take, these will never be steps you take and then leave behind. Almost all our sessions contain an element of worship, of listening to God proclaiming the Gospel, or outreach. Some of our sessions will focus on whichever specific aspect we feel we have been led towards. But now we are developing two junior leaders – both 11 years old – I have no doubt that they will be advising us adults on the direction we should be going in very soon.

The most important instructions, however, will always be God's. It is essential throughout that you listen to him and his specific instructions to you. The plans outlined here will never be a formula for success. They will simply be guidelines that could help you take the enormous step of faith in moving from a totally book-based Sunday school to a child-based church for which the only book is the Bible.

Do I really mean a child-based church? Yes. Not a child*ish* church, but one that accepts the basic generational premise that we are all equal in God's sight, regardless of age, etc., and that also accepts that we need to come to him like children. Remember, you can't get away from the fact that children had a special significance and importance to Jesus. He gave them a special place in his ministry because they had still been largely unaffected by society.

We take our children out into the world – prayer walking, having fun and meeting other children in the park. This is part of our outreach.

We are getting our children ready to start working in our schools. Not when we think they should, but when God tells them the time is right. We are seeking God's anointing for everything they do, so it is very important that they do their real outreach in his timing – not ours.

In a typical class of 30 children, 27 will not be active Christians. If only half those became Christians as a result of 'in-school' outreach, at least 13 would be going home to witness to their families. When Jesus was on earth, a number of people rejected him. So we have to accept that some of the children approached will not become Christians as a result of the young, evangelistic army. If only half the children approached became Christian, that would still leave six families converted as the result of one child's anointed evangelism in one class. It's like a giant snowball. As it gathers momentum it picks up even more and more snow until large numbers of a community have been gathered. One of the key teaching points I referred to is making sure that the children learn to have God's heart for the lost. This is why!

In a prayer meeting my wife was shown a mountain. At the top of the mountain God started a small snowball. As the snowball rolled down towards the people on the mountainside, they had to make a decision. They could stay in its path facing the snowball. This would allow them to hold onto it as it rolled over them, and so they would be swept up in it. They could turn away from it but remain in its path. This resulted in them being flattened by it as it passed over them. The snowball then carried on without them, or they could simply stand aside and let it pass by without it touching them in any way!

Reach out, children!

Always encourage the children in their outreach. They are out in the mission field planting seeds. It is their job to plant the seeds, not to make them grow. Only God can do that. If a child's evangelism does not *seem* to produce fruit – keep planting!

Some years ago I heard Reinhart Bonke talking about his ministry. He mentioned in the interview that God had told him that he would preach to one million people in one live mission. Those years ago that figure sounded ridiculously impossible. However, in November 2000, he had a mission in Nigeria during which he had over one-million people attend for four of the five nights he was there. That sounds an amazing testimony. To be able to stand at heaven's gates and say that he had taken God's word to over a million people on more than one occasion. But that is still a small vision when you think of all the people that the children of the world could reach! Most of the worst dictators in the world have young children in their families. Those children mix with other children! Their peers can reach those places that other peers cannot reach!

We would not even be allowed to stand outside the front door of a presidential palace, prime minister's home or home of an important international leader, etc., but certain children – close friends and relatives – have the total right of absolutely unobstructed access! Even Reinhart Bonke does not have that!

That is why I find this current move of God so exciting. Catch the vision and reap the harvest! But be warned. You could be blessed with the children from all walks of life.

I referred to the fact that changing your Sunday school programme could affect the whole church in ways they would never have expected. Now you can begin to see why! Jesus was condemned for talking to prostitutes, beggars, tax collectors and sinners. People from all walks of life will be saved, and if the children plant the seeds, then it will be the 'established church' – i.e. the adults – who will have to work with *and* lead to salvation all who are brought through our doors.

We are supposed to follow Jesus' example, so we can expect to receive similar criticisms. 'Oh, that's the church that all the down-and-outs go to. You don't want to go there!' Maybe you don't, but I know which church Jesus will show up in!

Prayer

Prayer is an area we often neglect as adults. Children who are brought up to pray will often go through the motions, but more to keep Mum or Dad happy than because they feel they have a real need. That is, until something happens! During the war there were three national days of prayer. If you check the dates of these days against the events of the war in your history books you will find something strange. The war took a major switch in direction within days of these prayer days – the most famous one being the day of prayer held a few days before the evacuation of Dunkirk. As we all know, the weather was abnormally calm and dry during that evacuation, and many lives were saved as a result!

There seems to have been no mention of holding a national day of prayer until another potential disaster hung over the British countryside – the outbreak of foot-and-mouth disease in 2000-2001. The suggestion was made when the outbreak was getting worse and worse. Then, quite suddenly the outbreak started to subside, so the government decided that a national day of prayer was not needed. Within days the outbreak flared up again!

When children have been moved to pray, they will pray with a fervour that leaves many adults behind! Have you ever tried to ignore the request of a child who is fervently asking for something? Now try to imagine God with his infinitely greater love than we have, trying to resist the fervent prayer of a child for his friends or his nation. Children's prayers are powerful prayers.

Children are a vital prayer force, and already there are stories coming in from children's workers who have been 'blown away' by the prayer of these children. In a report published in *Alive,* June 2001, Charmaine Ryan describes how the prayer force of children in a conference in Australia powerfully impacted everyone there. Some of her prayer warriors were only 5 years old!

The disciples asked Jesus how they should pray and they were given a prayer frame on which they could hang their own prayers. The frame helped the disciples to put the various 'prayer topics' into a correct priority order.

If children ask you how they should pray tell them to listen to God. If he shows them a direction in which he wants them to go, tell them to 'go for it'! But, go for it from the heart. Then pray from the heart again!

Remember, children's prayer priorities may be different from ours. Perhaps they will be better! On 11 September 2001, about 5000 people were killed by terrorists in the New York Trade Center disaster. This inspired worldwide prayer for America, and it caused a major response from Americans, some starting to attend church for the first time. The economic ramifications could go on for years. A major area for adult prayer!

Apparently an estimated 500,000 pregnancies are terminated in America every year. This is the type of topic that will often reduce praying children to tears! Not because of the economic effects – which they don't understand – but because they will feel the pain on God's heart as he watches 500,000 babies he has created being murdered.

When your children weep and wail during prayer – you will know that God is behind the prayer, and they are only reflecting his anguish! God may well anguish over aspects of life that many adults do not consider to be very important!

Going to the whole body experience!

First of all, there is no perfect Church. So you may decide to fully integrate your children and then find problems. If you don't find any, please let me know how you are doing it!

If you are expecting your children to provide you with the keys to the kingdom, you have to do something about it first. If you just let the children 'do their own thing' the comments you will get will encourage you to revert to children's church or even, dare I say – Sunday school – and keep them out of the way again!

When we started on this journey we didn't even know what road we were on! We just realised that our first priority had to be to work with *our own church children* before we even considered outreach, and bringing in new children. This was a totally new concept for us, and at that stage we had no idea where we were being led. We had a $1^1/_2$-hour session one evening each week at which we started to explore the avenues of Worship. At this time, children tended to 'do their own thing' in the main celebration and part of our role seemed to be quelling riots and sword fights that started when one child accidentally (at least, *he* said it was) bumped into another child!

Things did not happen immediately, but over a few weeks the children learned how to worship, how to listen to God, how to minister to others and so on. As the children's leaders we tended to gather a little flock around us in the main celebration, so we started *leading* them in worship dance. This involved the help of the worship leader who had to play one of the hymns with which the children were familiar. Familiar actions to a familiar hymn, following the lead of a familiar leader – in slightly unfamiliar surroundings. Only one hurdle to cross! By crossing these hurdles step by step their confidence has increased, so now they will worship and dance to unfamiliar hymns. Generally they still like to feel the presence of one of the leaders, but they will 'go it alone', and go in totally new directions when prompted by God or a leader. Ultimately, most of the children will feel able to keep with their parents throughout a service – except when led to dance or worship in a different way. Some, however, will always want to sit with a children's leader throughout the worship, as this will give them encouragement to worship with the other children. Children often get security sitting with their peers, especially when they know that their peers may start doing something that they want to join in with – and Mum and Dad are sitting 10 rows back!

We have learned through all this that the children really do need a training ground. But what's so odd about that! Training is available for our ministers, worship leaders, and a number of other offices in the church, why shouldn't children need some training before being let loose on the congregation?

Being IG friendly

So that is your next step. You can't just go from traditional church or children's church to IG church (intergenerational church) and expect it all to happen without any input from the leadership team. You will either need to have a weekly evening meeting for your church children, or keep them out of the main service perhaps every other week so that you can give them some intensive training. Always keep focused on *why* this is all so important and *what* you expect from the children.

As things develop you need the co-operation of the others in the service. There is no point in you training your children to be active members of the worship team (that is actually what they are, even if they never leave the congregation!) if the worship leader never plays the type of songs that inspires them to worship! There is nothing more disheartening than having your children 'all fired up', and then finding that all the worship hymns are not really suitable for dance worship. During one of these 'sedate' periods of worship we have had the question passed to us – 'Aren't the children doing anything this morning?' Unfortunately, if there are no suitable worship songs for a few weeks, the children will need a very firm prompting to get started again – so a lot of support from the worship leader is essential if it is to work!

With the best will in the world, an address can be boring for children. However, if you can find a quick sketch artist who can draw on OHP transparencies whilst the address is in progress, this will have a powerful effect on the children. These should be projected onto a wall or screen fairly close to, but behind the main speaker. This will keep everyone focused in the direction of the speaker.

Being an IG cell church, most of our children know that they will be expected to talk about the address in their cell meeting. Because of this they usually make notes. Their notes are usually based on what the 'artist' writes or draws on the OHP. We rotate this duty as we have no inspired artists, and I have often had children running out to me to copy the picture I have just replaced because they haven't quite finished the last one! It keeps them focused and paying attention. Sometimes a touch of humour on the OHP adds to the address – but not too much otherwise you can distract from it!

Speaking to children

Sometimes, however, you will have a speaker who, with the best will in the world, has no chance of holding the attention of the children for more than five minutes! When we get one of these we tend to take the children out of the main hall at the start of the address. We make sure that we have details of what the main speaker wants to say, then we present the meat from the message in a child-friendly way. So, although we try to keep our children in the main meeting most of the time we still take them out when we feel it necessary.

For years speakers have got used to the fact that children will not be present during their address. As a result, many sermons have developed into theological arguments that lose all the children and most of the adults!

When faced with an IG church, these speakers will feel out of their depth when suddenly having to confront a line of young faces or upturned bottoms! Speaking to an IG church meeting will be a new experience for most speakers, and many of them will need to be introduced slowly to the concept.

Children likewise. For years they have got into the 'mindset' that sermons are boring, and are just for adults! Sadly, our age of instant entertainment and the choice of instant TV has made the learning curve for children a much more difficult one to work within.

When D. L. Moody started the Sunday school movement, children were used to sitting down for long periods of time. Those who went to school were used to sitting in desks that made movement impossible. Those who did move about too much were quickly warned, and then 'firmly' made to sit still. The cane was a feature of every classroom, and it was often used.

All these things are from the past. Today schools do not teach children with formal discipline. Teachers are taught that if their class is not sitting still, it's the teacher's fault! The lesson is not exciting enough!

Even when relaxing the same lesson is taught. Most children have a whole range of games, computer games, hand-held electronic games, and a choice of television channels that they can flip between the second one programme starts to become even slightly boring!

For years we have been teaching our children that the second they start to become bored they can do something about it by pressing a button! We are now expecting these same children to sit through an address without getting bored with church! D. L. Moody had it easy compared to the preachers of this generation!

However, don't forget God! He is well aware of the enormous difficulties we are facing. He knows that if we just relied on our own efforts to draw these children into his kingdom, and into the IG church situation – we would have no chance of success, and within another generation church could be dead! That, I am certain, is not in God's plan! Already I have heard stories of young children praying – from choice – for over an hour. In other countries where, I accept, the social pressure of affluence doesn't exist as it does here, children are willingly giving their lives to be martyred rather than deny the name of Jesus. This is happening quite regularly in Indonesia. That is not the result of a child thinking through the consequences of their actions. It is not the result of a child trying to win friends! This is only possible if that child has a real and deep relationship with Jesus! That has not come through teaching, but through experience!

I believe that what this is all about is that God is about to speak to his children on a worldwide basis. Children are the fuel of the next revival. All we are doing through the current changes that are going on is facilitating this situation.

God spoke to Samuel very directly and very clearly four times. On the first three occasions Samuel had no idea who was speaking, and he went through to the priest, Eli, believing that it was Eli who had called him. Samuel had not been prepared to hear the voice of God. It was not until Eli finally switched on his dormant spiritual brain and gave Samuel a 'last minute lesson' in hearing the voice of God that he was able to tell Samuel what to do!

We are not going to make the same mistake with our children. Our children will have learned how to worship, how to pray, and how to hear the voice of God long before it becomes a crisis situation.

Ministry

Part of the training we have given our children has included ministry, both from a child-to-child and a child-to-adult basis. We usually have a sensitive leader who will go to the side of our hall during ministry time, from where they will be dispatched to help pray for people, take tissues to people who need them. They can also take cloths to cover the legs of people who feel the need to lie down during the ministry. So they are positively and effectively used. The prayers of the children are welcomed by the adults. At a recent prophetic conference it was some of the children who spoke into situations more effectively than the adults!

Organisational ideas

When you have teachers who are used to leaving the main body of the church half-way through the service so that they can teach the children for 20-30 minutes only, the step from that to having the children for the whole service is a big step. If your teachers are reluctant to take that step, you could start off with a short programme just to prove that Sunday school without books works. The only problem with this is the one I have already referred to. Some people will not be committed, and will not make a serious effort. They will be looking for the opportunity to tell you that they knew it wouldn't work. 'So let's go back to where we were! We were safe and comfortable there!'

A sermon slot: 20-30 minutes

The next few ideas are there to give you some guidance should you be required to cover a sermon slot of perhaps 20-30 minutes, which is possibly on the short side for an effective time with the children.

Once things 'took off' in Pensacola, it is worth noting that a light system was installed so that a message could be sent between the children's meeting and the adults meeting so that some co-ordination could be introduced. But, the final control was given to the children's meeting – not the adults! If the children had not finished what they were doing, then the minister or worship team had to keep the adults occupied until the children were ready!

Session 1

You could select a good worship song such as 'Who paints the skies'. Project the words onto a wall so that the children can see them without having pieces of paper to get in the way. Play the tape or CD, and ask the children to just follow the words for the first time through. Then play the tape a second time, and one of the leaders will have to lead the children in possible actions as suggested by the words in the song. Get the children to copy. (It's a fun song, they'll enjoy it!). Look at some of the words they may not understand. What is the song saying?

Move onto a second song. Perhaps 'You are my passion'. (It's on the same CD as 'Who paints the skies' – see notes at the end of this book.) The tempo is totally different in this hymn. How do the children feel they should worship in this one? (Discuss.) Try it – but you will still have to have an adult leader for them to follow. As you worship, watch the children to see if you have any inspired worshippers. You could have some emerging this early!

You could return to the first song and see if there is anyone else who would like to lead. The actions are so easy to follow that you could have several volunteers. Give each one about 15-20 seconds to lead, then ask the next volunteer to take over.

You will have to keep a careful eye on the time as you could find time runs out at a crucial point. If there is time, you could ask everyone to sit down and tell you what they think God thinks about the two songs you have used. Did he enjoy you singing them? Did he enjoy their worship? Tell them about David dancing before the ark as it entered Jerusalem.

Session 2

Start with 'Who paints the skies', but only play it through once. (They may object to this, so promise them a rerun at the end of the session.) Then possibly 'Great big God'. Again something totally different! Depending on your group you may be able to use the children to lead, but you will probably still need adult leaders for another week or so.

Get the children to lie down, close their eyes and think about what this Great Big God might be saying to them. They should write down their answers, or dictate them to a leader.

End with 'Who paints the skies'.

I could easily develop these ideas and write a series of 10 easy lessons to lead your children to God. But as soon as I start taking this theme further I am giving you a book! So, for Session 3, and all subsequent sessions – *pray*, see where God has led you during the first two sessions and use the frame above to plan where you are being led next!

Planning a longer session

If you have more time to work with, then you will have much more freedom. Some churches that run a 'children's church' have the children delivered to the children's section right a the start of the service. This seems a shame, but there are often very good practical reasons why churches keep their children totally separate. Other churches now start their services with 30-45 minutes of worship which the children join in with. These churches sometimes keep the children in for all the worship, or will send the little children out just before the worship goes especially deep. These deeper sessions of worship can lead into a time of ministry, and some people find the youngest children a distraction during ministry. But don't forget that ministry is equally important for the younger children. It is very easy to treat the crèche leadership as the 'baby minding' group! Forget it! The little ones can be ministered to through carefully chosen taped music, they can be told stories about Jesus. They can learn to talk to Jesus and they can be prayed for and prayed over. There is a real ministry with the under-5s, who often reach the age of 5 without ever hearing stories about Jesus.

As the leader of the children you can expect to have the children for an hour or so. As the children enter the children's area it can be quite refreshing to have a very short 'pit stop' for a drink and a biscuit. A typical children's church programme would then possibly be:

The Welcome

This is the time where any new children will be introduced. Each child may then tell everyone something good that has happened to them during the previous week. The welcome can be short or extended depending on circumstances. Groups should be of about 12 children. The natural tendency would be for these groups to be based on age groups, but I would suggest that they should deliberately be arranged across the entire age range. You may prefer to have a range of three to four years in each group, so that the youngest children and the oldest are not together. This is important for the development and growth of the children whereas the traditional age grouping tends to be for the convenience of the teacher!

Worship

Depending on how much, if any, they have had in the main meeting there should now be some worship along the lines given above for the shorter session.

The Word

The word section should be based on the main reading and theme being used in the grown-ups' meeting. Ministers should provide the children's leaders with the key points, main readings, and the main points they want to get across to the adults at least a day in advance, and preferably three to four days in advance. This gives the children's leaders a chance to review the material and to see how they are being led to present it to the children.

They will also be able to develop applications for the children that are real to them. For example, in a main address based on 'You shall not steal', the preacher may dwell on misappropriation of office paper-clips, postage stamps, and the incorrect tax returns some people make! Clearly references that are not applicable to children. However, taking something from another child's bag at school, sweets from the counter at the sweet shop, or money from Mum's purse are areas that are directly relevant to children. Have you ever tried to explain to an 8-year-old about 'not coveting his neighbour's wife or maidservant'?

There will be a tendency to group the children by age, but with the exception of the under-5s, you can have a lot of success keeping all the primary aged children in one group, or of having vertical groups where age does not matter. Even young teenagers can fit into these vertical groups with great success, and they will often take on extra responsibilities within the 'family' group, such as looking after and helping the younger children in the group. Helping to organise the worship, possibly playing instruments for live worship.

Witness

Children are no longer being slowly prepared for when they grow up. They are being prepared for God's army of today, so they will need to start thinking of what *they* can do to help bring God's word to the lost. Talking these issues through, with the children doing most of the talking, will give them a lot of encouragement. Who can they witness to? How can they do it?

Age grouping

If the children are expected to join the main body of the church at the age of 11 or 12, then an 'age free' family group can be very effective. The older ones can be given extra responsibility within the group, and they will naturally look after the younger ones. It also avoids the problem that can be caused when a number of the older ones 'get together'.

However, if the teenage children also have a group to go to certain questions can now be asked.

1. Do you want the children to 'leave' their secure family group at 11 or 12?
2. Do you want a family group to include teenagers?
3. Do your leaders want to work with children within the 5-16 age range within the same family group?

4. Would your leaders like to take on a group of about 12 that they would see right through to about 16?
5. If the idea of staying with a group could be useful, would a three-year age band work more effectively?
6. If this has possibilities, how are you going to cope with the fluctuating numbers, especially during the first two years of any group?

A possible programme

The following programme of five sessions may help to get you started.

Session 1

Warm up or Welcome

Sit in circles of up to 15 children in each. Each circle to have a small, soft cushion or a bean bag. Toss the cushion gently to someone else in the group who must catch it, then give their name and tell everyone something nice that has happened during the past week.

Worship

Start by getting the children to sit in an open space so that they can see the words of the songs you are projecting onto the wall/screen. Now play an exciting worship hymn such as 'Who paints the skies', or 'Lord, I lift your name on high', etc. Play the chosen hymn again, but this time one leader should stand at the front and interpret the words and music through their movements. Get the children to join in, copying the actions of the leader. Repeat, using the same song but a different leader. It will be especially helpful if one leader is male. The children copy again, but this time they will notice a number of differences. That is good. We're not leading up to a dance routine but dance in worship!

Repeat, but this time use a different hymn with a different tempo. This time use a much quieter hymn. Again the children should just copy the actions of the appointed leader.

Word

This presumes that you have not been given a text from the adult speaker. In each circle group look at a prepared list of the gifts of the Spirit (See 1 Corinthians 12:7-11). What do they mean? Talk about how we (adults and children) can use each of these gifts. Give the children a picture of Jesus using the gifts to colour or let them draw their own if they would prefer to. When are these gifts for? Who are these gifts for? Are they for us? Discuss all these issues with the children.

Witness

If these gifts are for us, what should we do about it? Draw out from the children that we should be seeking these gifts by praying for them, asking for them, by being with people who are blessing others as they use these gifts (with older groups refer to Mark 16:15-18).

Prayer

Pray that God will bless the children with these gifts as he has promised to.

Closing prayer

At an appropriate moment, close the meeting with a prayer. If you have finished the meeting early you could let the children continue with their pictures until the adults are ready, or perhaps organise a simple game.

When you pray, just talk as though Jesus was standing just in front of you. Don't use thee's and thou's, etc. You wouldn't talk to your human parent that way, would you? The children may well copy your example – when perhaps you should be copying theirs!

Session 2

Warm up

Sit in circles of 15 or less. Give your name and then name a fruit or animal whose name begins with the same letter (or sound, with lower infants).

If you could be any fruit, what fruit would you like to be and why?

Worship

Start by playing the most popular hymn played in Session 1, and expect them to copy the leader for the first time through. Play the same hymn again, but this time pick children to take the lead for about 15-20 seconds each. Don't stop the music, just call out the name of the child you want everyone else to follow. Play a second hymn – possibly 'Lord, you have my heart, and I will search for yours'. The leader should lead, using a much more intimate style of worship. Again, the children can copy the leader, but children who are already displaying their own intimate worship can be encouraged to continue doing their own thing. Flags or lengths of material can be brought in to aid the worship. With practice even infants can worship sensibly and safely – but don't expect immediate success! The difficult lesson is getting the children to learn that you can still be worshipping with flags . . . even when the flags are lying on the floor!

(Sometimes we give 'children's' hymns or other simple hymns that we think will go well to children – and we get it wrong! Be prepared to adjust the type of hymns you use, either because the children respond better to more 'adult' hymns, or because as they grow in the Lord, their choice of hymns might change.

Word

Working in the circular groups again, look at the list of spiritual gifts that you looked at in Session 1. Recap on what these gifts mean, and think about which gift you would like to ask for. (Ask and it shall be given to you, seek and you shall find.) If God offered us these gifts – why don't we all have them? What gets in the way? Why did Jesus have to die?

From this, you should find that 'sin' gets in the way. Get the children to draw a picture of themselves committing a sin they often commit – or write down all the sins they can think of that they are guilty of. Emphasise that only they and Jesus will ever know what they have written and total honesty is necessary if God is to bless their actions. When they have finished, ask them to fold up or screw up all the pieces of paper and put them in the middle of the circle. Ask God to forgive them for those sins. Then accept his forgiveness, and destroy the pieces of paper. (Burning them is very effective, but not always possible.) This may sound heavy, but it is important. Any objections will come from adults – who usually make much more of this type of exercise than the children! Children really enjoy this activity – especially if the papers can be burned. They get a great feeling of freedom from it. Adult leaders should *always* join in fully with these exercises.

Witness

In the Lord's Prayer it says, 'Forgive us . . . as we forgive others . . .' Get the children to repeat the previous exercise, but this time they write down or draw pictures to show the way other people have hurt or upset them. This time when the pieces of paper go into the middle everyone prays forgiveness over the people mentioned, and again, the pieces of paper should be destroyed without being read.

Prayer

Praying over these pieces of paper can be corporate with everyone praying a general prayer aloud. Praying in the Spirit so only the person praying and God know the problem, or silent 'heart' prayers.

Some people have difficulty forgiving others. If you become aware of this problem ask those having difficulty to ask Jesus to help them to forgive those people they are having difficulty forgiving. *Or* they could write the sins they need to forgive on a balloon, which they can then burst. This is another particularly enjoyable exercise.

Closing prayer

If possible, end with the hymn 'My shackles are gone', then let the children get together for some favourite games.

Session 3

Warm up

Sit in your circle groups. The leader starts by naming any animal that starts with the letter *a*. The next person names one beginning with the letter *b* and so on around the group. If someone gets stuck the leader calls out *towns*, or *pop groups*, or *football teams*, etc., and the person who was stuck either continues with the same letter, but the new subject grouping, or you can revert to *a* again. This could be made competitive by making sure that the leader in each circle has the same list of groupings, and each leader makes a note of how far through the alphabet they get before getting stuck.

Worship

Display a list of the Spiritual gifts, and play two or three hymns, starting with a popular and lively one, but ending on a reflective note. Give each child a piece of paper and a pencil, ask them to write their name on it and ask them to lie face down, arms folded under their heads, and eyes shut.

Play quiet background Christian music, preferably music without words. Whilst the music is playing, ask the children to imagine a scene such as the following:

Imagine you are lying in a field, the pleasantly hot sun is shining on you, and you could easily go to sleep, but you can hear someone coming. The field slopes down to a large lake, and as you watch a tall man with a beard, and wearing long white robes approaches you. You recognise him immediately as Jesus. He squats down on the grass next to you and calling you by your favourite name he says hello. He then asks if there is anything you would like to ask him.

Tell him that you have heard about his gifts and tell him which one you would especially like. Look at Jesus' face and listen to his answer. When you have one, write this on your piece of paper.

(Younger children will need help with the writing.) Children should write their names on their papers so that you can look after them.

Now ask him which gift he most wants to give you to use.

The answers may be different!

Word

Look through the New Testament and find three different questions that different people asked Jesus when he was on earth. Look at the story of the woman at the well (John 4:4-26). Look at her question. Draw and colour the picture of her talking to Jesus. Which gift did Jesus use to answer her?

Witness

Jesus showed you which gifts he most wanted you to have. Jesus gives us gifts so that we can use them with other people. Ask the children how each of them is going to use their gifts when they are working or playing with other children, or when they are at home.

Prayer-request box

Set up a prayer-request box, and ask the children and adults to put prayer requests into the box. They can put in more than one. (At the end of the session check to make sure that you have at least as many prayer requests as there are people. If there are too few, add a few general prayer requests for the nation, major leaders, etc. Explain to the children that they will use these prayer requests in the next session.

Prayer

Pray to receive the gifts that God wants to give you and for the faith to use them.

Closing prayer

Close in prayer thanking God for his gifts.

Session 4

Warm up

Sit in circles of up to 15 people and play 'I sent a letter to my friend'. One person walks around the circle and touches someone who is sitting down. The person touched has to get up and catch the toucher before s/he can run around the circle and sit in the place of the person who was touched (i.e. they both have to run a full circuit of the circle).

Worship

a) Ask the children to listen to the words of 'Father, you have given' otherwise called 'Ambassadors of reconciliation' or a similar hymn. Just think about the words. If possible play a recording of that hymn.
b) If you can get a recording of 'The Spirit of the Sovereign Lord is upon me', talk about the words and what they mean.
c) Ask the children to lie down and listen to the words and music as you play them.

Word

Look at where the words of the song you have just played occur in the Bible (Luke 4:18 and Isaiah 61:1). Think about their significance. Relate these words to the children today. We can also claim these words because of the Christ who lives in us.

Talk about our responsibilities and in twos or threes pray for each other seeking acknowledgement for our individual role, and asking God to help us use our God-given gifts wisely.

Witness

Play 'I sent a letter to a friend' again – only for a few moments. Talk about the way the 'letter' was delivered. This is like the delivery of a prayer handkerchief!

Play 'Pass the parcel' *but* the parcel you pass will contain a small sweet at *every* layer – including the last one, and it will contain a prayer request from the prayer box at every layer. Tell the children how important this 'game' is – both for the person being prayed for *and* the person saying the prayer – as God will make sure that the parcel stops at the right place so that the 'right' person delivers the prayer. As a layer is removed the child opening the parcel reads the prayer request. If possible they lead a short prayer in answer to that request – or a leader can help them. Prayers must be short. The child then 'wins' the sweet. Try to make sure that there are more layers in your parcel than there are children, and that every child gets at least one chance to pray. (Either control the music carefully, or if the parcel stops with someone who has already said a prayer, they should pass it to the next person in the circle who has not yet prayed.)

Closing prayer

Thank God for the opportunity of being able to pray for friends, and thank him for the gift of prayer for others in intercession.

Session 5

Warm up

a) Sit in a circle of about 15 people; one should have a soft ball or cushion, etc. On the command, the person with the 'ball' gets up and runs around the circle until s/he gets back to his/her place. As s/he sits down s/he passes the ball to his/her left. The ball is passed the whole way around the circle until it reaches the person on the right of the first person. That person gets to his/her feet and runs around the circle until s/he gets back to his/her place, when they also pass the ball to the left . . . and so on until everyone has had a turn. The first team to finish is the winner. If you only have a small group, make a square of roughly equal sides. Each side has a ball, but this time the runner starts at one end of his side and runs the whole way around until he reaches the other end of the line. He then passes the ball along the line. When it reaches the other end the new runner gets up and runs, and everyone slides along a place to leave a place for the new runner to sit in.

b) Ask the group to answer the question, 'If an angel appeared in the middle of the group now, and he told you that he could answer one question, what question would you ask him?'

Worship

Play three or four different hymns. The first one should be very noisy, but the tempo should drop as you progress through the list to the last, a very slow hymn. Ask the children to worship in any way they like, but they must vary their style of worship as they flow from hymn to hymn. As they finish the last hymn, drop the volume and ask them to lie on their tummies, arms stretched forward and eyes closed. As they lie there, tell them to imagine that they are walking through a curtain into the Throne room, and Jesus is sitting on a big throne in front of them. Try to create an impression of absolute grandeur and majesty but use very few words. Let them lie and worship in silence for a few moments. When you feel the time is right, tell them to roll over and sit up. Ask them how they felt and if they 'saw' anything. Write down everything they saw.

Spend some time thanking God for what he showed the children.

Word

Give the children a piece of paper and a pencil. Remind the children about the specific gifts of the Spirit (1 Corinthians 12:7-11) and remind them that these are not the only gifts. Read Romans 12:8. What are these spiritual gifts? Which of these do they think they have? Write down the answer. Which would they like? Write down the answer. Get the children into threes and ask them to pray for each other, asking God to give the person they are praying for the specific gift they have asked for.

Now repeat the whole process, but this time asking for the gifts of the Spirit that each child wants. Again, group them in threes and ask them to pray for each other asking God to give the child being prayed for the gift they have requested.

Tell the children to accept the gifts in faith, and thank God for giving each of them their chosen gift.

Witness

Read Mark 16:15-18. All these gifts have been offered to us to help us fulfil the Great Commission. This is to bring the Gospel message to all nations and to bring glory to the name of God. Tell the children to take their giftings into their schools, families, etc., and to do their best to fulfil the last instruction Jesus gave us. If time permits, talk about how they could do this. What problems could they encounter, and how should they face up to them?

Closing prayer

Thank God for his many gifts and ask for the wisdom and guidance needed for us to use them wisely.

How to use these notes

These five drafted lesson plans could be used exactly as they have been written. They have been used in that form during a children's holiday scheme. When we were asked to run a children's conference recently we took the same programme, but changed it as we felt God wanted us to. With our own children in our home church it has taken us several months to work through the same material! So these plans are simply there to give you something to lean on as you get started on this new adventure!

Peter walked on the water – but we often forget that the other disciples stayed in the boat! Stepping out in faith is not easy, and these little plans may help you to step out onto the water and do what Peter failed to do all the time. To fasten his eyes on Jesus!

I could easily have extended these ideas and written a series of 25 easy lessons to lead your children to God. But as soon as I start taking this theme further I am giving you another book! Exactly what I am trying to avoid! If you have a book you will lean on the book . . . and not on God!

What about your children's pastor? If you are not having Sunday school each week you won't need a children's pastor, will you? Look at the money the church will save! (I bet someone says that in some churches!) Don't you believe it! There will be just as much work for the pastor to do, and soon there will be a lot more as the children start to bring in the harvest! Children need just as much 'after-conversion' care as adults!

Other tools or aids you could use

There are a few other tools that can be used, but use them with great care. They will never be formulae for success. They *will* work, and God *will* bless them – but only if you use them in response to his call, and you don't try to engineer things.

The river

We have a long piece of blue material. This is our 'river'. Sometimes we ask the children to lie in it, under it or stand on it. We have lifted it up and carried it over the congregation, or held it up and invited the congregation to go under it. All these actions can be very powerful, and can carry a very heavy anointing – but only if done in response to God's call.

The fire

We also have a bright red/orange-coloured cloth that we use to represent God's fire. We use this in the same way that we use the river.

The use of both of these items is rarely planned. We usually keep them in a bag in the main meeting – only to be used when prompted. Occasions may be weeks or months apart.

Prayer tunnel

This can be another very powerful experience, when members of the ministry team – adults and children – form an arch in the way that some people do for the bride at a wedding. The congregation is then invited to go slowly through the tunnel, each member of the ministry tunnel praying for each person going through.

Where to next?

Over the past year or so God has given me a number of pictures. As we started to go along this new work God showed me a road with houses on either side. In front of me was a gate. The houses stopped in line with the gate, and beyond the gate was open countryside. At this point I believe God was saying, 'Are you prepared to open the gate and go through it? Many will stop at the gate and want to remain in their known security, but I am seeking people who will walk through.'

Some time later I was brought back to the open countryside I was walking through, and I realised that the road had dwindled to a track and the track was about to stop. At this point I felt God was saying, 'The established road no longer exists. But will you press on, even though you cannot see the path ahead?'

Weeks later I was taken to the same scene, and as I was picking my way over the heath I felt God say, 'Look up! Many people will get this far but will still keep their eyes fastened on where they believe the track ought to be. Where I am leading is in the third dimension. You must look up towards me. Up here there is no track, only me to guide you.'

Some time later I was shown a room with a doorway, and it was strange because although the room I was in was light, no visible light could enter the doorway. It was like a force field in a science fiction programme. This time I felt God say to me, 'Are you prepared to go up to that doorway when you can't see what's beyond it?'

A few days later I found myself much closer to the doorway, and then on the edge of it, and I was being asked to trust God for everything. So I got ready to step into the apparent blackness, and as I prepared to step I was allowed to see some stepping stones that were on huge pillars rising out of the darkness. The top of the pillars glowed, and the very top step was glowing gold. As I stepped onto the stepping stones I felt totally safe and secure, and the further I stepped the more stepping stones I could see in front of me. So each step of the way God was not only holding my hand, but he was also showing me exactly where to step – one step at a time!

That gave me great encouragement, but it also means that I am only being allowed to see where to go next, step by step. I believe the same applies to you. If you have the courage to embark on this journey, God will show you each step you have to take and when you should take it. In that way you will always be dependent on him rather than on your judgement and plans.

A few months ago we had a gifted prophet come to our church. She knew nothing about me or what I did, but she prophesied that I would be writing material that would help people working with children to lead their charges to Jesus!

Don't let the vision grow dim

When we were half-way through the programme and we were not quite sure which way to go next, my wife did her daily Bible study and found that it was about 'not letting the vision grow dim'. So she prayed and asked God to show her where to go next. I quote from her journal:

> Now is the time for the teaching. You have instilled in my children the fact that they can talk to me and hear from me. They know that I have plans for them and they know that it may be costly for them to follow me.
>
> Now teach them why I need them. Teach them of the 'Great Commission', teach them of my heart for the lost, my love for all mankind. Then show them the Scriptures about my rewards for them – the eternal riches that are theirs.
>
> Finally teach them how to fulfil this task. How to become mighty warriors with my power and authority at their disposal – I will do the rest! [What a promise!]
>
> Don't keep looking at the negative, the 'what ifs', don't see them in the flesh, but see them as I see them. Little volcanoes waiting to burst open and pour out fire and unstoppable energy. Don't you believe I can do it?
>
> 'Well yes, Lord, but can I?'
>
> 'You can't! Fortunately, you don't have to! I AM and I CAN and I WILL!'

So the simple answer to the question I started this section with has to be – I don't know! I have the vision – which I see as rather like having had a very quick glance at a completed jigsaw picture. I have had a glance and I can remember aspects of the picture that really impacted me, but there is a lot of detail that didn't register. I have pieces of the puzzle, and with God's help have managed to fit some of them together – so I am beginning to see – in detail – small sections of the picture. But there is still a lot I cannot see. I hope I have managed to share with you the vision for the whole picture, but you have read it second-hand. You cannot ever see that aspect as clearly as I do, but God will show you your section of the picture far more clearly than he has shown me. Your steps may be similar to mine. Indeed, they could be very similar – but they will still be different. However, they could be very different from mine . . . once you have left the road and sought his path!

There have been times when we have openly said, 'We don't know where we are going next!' But that's good. God is in the driving seat! We have seen our children rise to wonderful new heights – and do you know what? We ain't seen nothing yet!

We know our children are going to fly! God is going to take them to heights that will make them dizzy! But through it, they will bring such a blessing and such a harvest to the Church.

I know I am repeating myself, but it really is important that you never see these ideas as a formula for success.

When we started on this road we could find nothing to help us. There were a number of books that told us God was doing a new thing – well, we knew that! We had heard that traditional Sunday school was on its way out – well, we'd guessed that! But what next? Were we alone in our efforts to find a solution? We certainly seemed to be!

Be encouraged. You are not alone! If you are stepping out on this new road there will be times when you wonder . . . but be encouraged – we have all done that! There will be times when others wonder, and they may try to talk you out of it . . . but be encouraged – we've all had that! There will be times when you wonder – 'What next Lord?' . . . but be encouraged. We've all said that!

I believe we are on the edge of the biggest true revival ever! If we know it – then I'm certain that the devil does too! Doubts will be planted at every turn to make you pull back – but don't! Be encouraged. Jesus did not promise us an easy journey, or even an easy life – but he did promise enormous rewards! So be encouraged and go for it!

Questions for moving forward

If you are thinking of making changes, there are a number of questions you will need to ask and stages you will need to go through. A few have been printed below to help you focus on the main issues. However, this is not the finite list of all questions and steps! You will have others. Just add them to this list.

1. Before you start – pray! God may give you an answer before you've asked the question!
2. Do you really want to go for it? (It may seem obvious, but must be answered!)
3. Is the children's leader fully committed?
4. Does the church leader/minister support your quest?
5. Now draft out a possible Sunday programme *as you see it!*
6. Are enough of the children's helpers on board and supportive?
7. With these helpers, develop your Sunday programme for the children.
8. What changes will this make to the main celebration?
9. Will these changes create major problems?
10. Can you see any solutions?
11. You have ironed out as many of the problems as you can; do you still want to proceed?
12. If you do, take your plans, problems and solutions to the minister.
13. With the minister, work through a service step by step to try to uncover any hidden problem.
14. Present your final draft for consideration or a trial run.

The armies and their armour!

On the next pages we have reproduced two songs through which our children have enjoyed worshipping God. They are easy to physically 'act' to, and will help the children to learn Ephesians 6. The words have been reproduced so that they can easily be photocopied onto an OHP sheet. The music is also included and this also may be photocopied for use by anyone who owns a copy of this book.

Music is very important in worship, and this often involves photocopying words and music for projection, etc. With photocopying restriction applying to most published words and music, and licences needing to be bought before music or words can be reproduced, the composers have requested that normal licensing requirements be lifted from the music on the following pages. As we believe that both these songs (one especially) were written with divine guidance, we cannot claim a copyright on something that belongs to God!

'Catch the Fire – 6. In Majesty He Rides' contains most of the tracks I have referred to.

Other music books that may help you:

Kidsource and *Kidsource 2* published by Kevin Mayhew.

The Source and *The Source 2* – music and words – Kevin Mayhew.

The army of God

Shake the dust from your bones,
look to Jesus alone,
let him clothe you in his armour bright.
With his sword in his hand
he will ride through the land
calling out to the army of God.

As you stand beside me,
watch the enemy flee
as we march side by side into battle.
Keep your mind fixed on God,
go where my feet have trod,
and we'll march as the army of God.

No more bondage to sin,
as the battle we win
over Satan and all of our foes.
He will set us all free,
we will have victory,
as we march in the army of God.

Chorus

Jesus' power as our source,
an unbeatable force,
rank by rank with our weapons held high.
Not a sound but the beat
of the marching of feet,
the invincible army of God.

Chorus

THE ARMY OF GOD

Jackie Smith

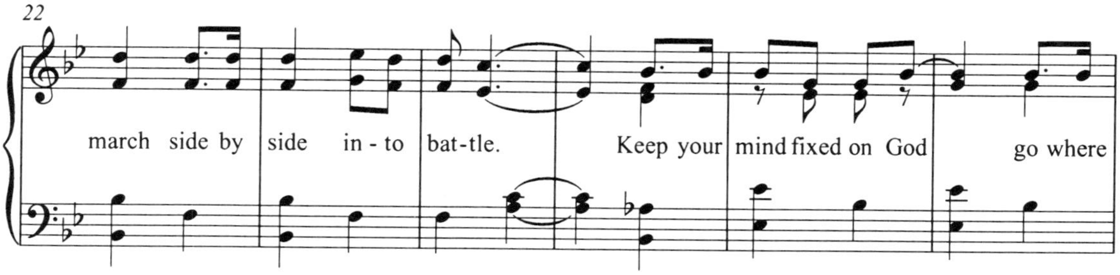

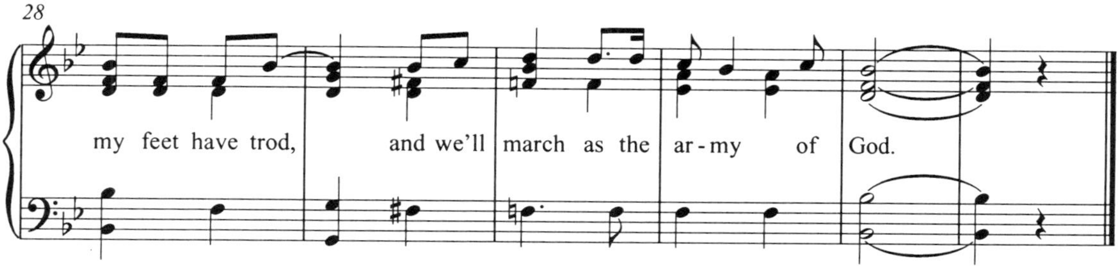

This music may be photocopied.

Be strong in the Lord

Ephesians 6:10, 11, 13-17

Be strong in the Lord and his mighty power,
put on the full armour of God.
For every moment of every hour,
start wearing the armour of God.
The battle we fight for the forces of light
it's a battle that Jesus has won.
The enemy's goal is to capture lost souls
so keep wearing the armour of God.

With the belt of truth buckled firm to your waist,
that's the start of the armour of God.
With the breastplate of righteousness firmly in place,
wear more of the armour of God.
With your feet marching forward in the Gospel of peace,
you can move in the armour of God.
In addition to this take the shield of your faith and
build up the protection of God.

With salvation's helmet firm on your head,
you're wearing the armour of God.
With the sword of the Spirit tight in your hand
you are part of the army of God!
The battle we fight for the forces of light,
it's a battle that Jesus has won.
As the enemy's goal is to capture lost souls
keep wearing the armour of God,

Put on the armour day by day
and we'll serve in the army of God!

BE STRONG IN THE LORD

Peter Smith

Based on Ephesians 6:10, 11, 13-17

Animé Alla Marcia

This music may be photocopied.